POWER TOOLS

chapter 10 p. 125

THE BUSINESS TOOL KIT

POWER TOOLS

TOP EXECUTIVE COACHES PUT YOU ON THE FAST TRACK TO SUCCESS

Ann E. Mah • Kristin Scott
Jolene A. Savage • Karen L. Anderson
Charles A. Breeding • David E. Nelson
Cynthia B. Stotlar • Glenn Daughtridge
Deb Clifford • Patricia Varley • Kate Zabriskie
Jim Peal • Bill Fotsch • Meg Montford • Valerie Simpson
Jonathan Clark• Ben Adkins • Susan Meyer-Miller • Daniel R. Fecht

COMPASS
SERIES PUBLISHING

For information contact:
Compass Series Publishing
3351 SE Meadowview Dr.
Topeka, KS 66605-3022
1-785-266-9434
Email: ann@compassseries.com
Web: www.CompassSeries.com

ISBN # 0-9754076-1-9
FIRST EDITION

Quality Compass Series Publishing℠ Books:

Power Tools: Top Executive Coaches Put You on the Fast Track to Success

Life Compass for Women:
The Indispensable Guidebook on Life Management for Busy Women

Career Compass for Women:
The Indispensable Guidebook for Women in the Workplace

TABLE OF CONTENTS

SECTION I: Essential Tools

TABLE OF CONTENTS

SECTION II: Tools to Build Winning Teams

TABLE OF CONTENTS

SECTION III: Tools for High Impact Leadership

INTRODUCTION

If you ever wondered what CEOs know that you don't, you've come to the right place. Hard work and technical skill can only take you so far up the corporate ladder. Those who rise to the executive levels have exceptional leadership and people skills. They know how to accomplish company goals through others. They have refined communications skills. They have an eye for detail, but are focused on the big picture. *Power Tools* is your guide to the skills you need to get to the executive suite. Written by top executive coaches and corporate trainers from all around the country, it is packed with the latest in business tools.

Each chapter is a mini-workshop full of thought-provoking ideas to help you take stock of your executive potential and gain the skills needed to succeed. Each chapter provides valuable tools you can use immediately to build a better career path. There is no need to read this book front to back. Choose the topic that intrigues you most and start there.

The book is divided into three sections: Essential Tools, Tools to Build Winning Teams, and Tools for High Impact Leadership. Essential Tools covers a variety of skills all executives need. Tools to Build Winning Teams gives you the communication and supervisory skills needed to deal effectively with your employees. High Impact Leadership asks you to dig deeper for greater understanding of the key tools great leaders know and use.

I hope you find *Power Tools* enjoyable as well as helpful. Let it be your business tool kit for building a successful career!

Ann E. Mah
Co-author and Editor
Owner – Compass Series Publishing

POWER TOOLS

SECTION I

Essential Tools

CHAPTER ONE

When People Don't Play Well With Others Your Career Suffers

Smart conflict resolution skills for smart leaders

Ben Adkins

Ben Adkins is nationally known in the areas of *leadership development*, *workplace conflict resolution,* and *personal effectiveness*. Since 1985 he has presented more than 2,800 workshops, seminars, keynotes, training classes and management retreats.

Ben educates, entertains, and involves audiences while providing practical, step-by-step instruction in an environment where participants both laugh and learn. He coaches executives and managers how to be more effective in their professional relationships and how to be a *leader* instead of a *boss*.

Ben's background includes executive management with a national distribution company and founder of two successful businesses in Chicago and Dallas. In 1985 he co-founded Adkins & Associates which provides *tools for increased effectiveness*. His clients include Fortune 500 companies, small and medium size organizations, and city, state and federal government organizations.

As an experienced mediator and conflict resolution specialist, Ben helps organizations create highly productive and profitable environments by strategically managing workplace conflict. His clients eliminate costly grievances, lawsuits and EEO complaints by resolving conflicts on the lowest levels.

Adkins & Associates
Fort Worth, TX • 817-370-8746 • www.TrainingSpeaking.com

Ben Adkins

When People Don't Play Well With Others Your Career Suffers

Smart conflict resolution skills for smart leaders

Ray is a manager whose career is stuck. He has been passed over for promotions, left out of the loop and perceived as ineffective. Why? Ray is technically skilled, dedicated and works hard to support his family. But, he has a critical skill deficit. He doesn't manage conflict well and this has resulted in poor performance by his staff. Many managers' careers have been derailed for this same reason. Don't let it happen to you.

Business is about building relationships. Your ability to manage workplace conflict is crucial to your leadership success and the quality of those relationships. Getting things done in the most effective way depends on the relationship you have with your co-workers, subordinates and bosses. When interpersonal conflicts spin out of control, they affect relationships in ways that create business problems. These problems include productivity declines, loss of good people, lawsuits, grievances, and worse. All of those things were happening in Ray's department.

The Good News

Conflict happens in the normal course of doing business and working together. Some conflicts are not bad and, indeed, could be good. For example, conflicts related to tasks, services, products or processes often lead to the discovery of better methods and lay the groundwork for positive change.

Some conflicts are simply business problems to be solved—the challenges we face. Examples are dealing with unexpected crises, scheduling problems, being short-staffed, trying to make a deadline, vendor or contractor problems, and many other day-to-day challenges we are paid to handle. Effective leaders are revealed when the pressure is on and challenges must be met. Smart leaders see performance conflicts as problem-solving opportunities and as stimuli for improvement.

The Bad News

Relationship conflicts have negative results. When conflicts go unresolved between people in interdependent relationships, there is an infectious tension created in the workplace that erodes productivity and vitality.

These are relationship conflicts rather than performance or process related conflicts. They can be peer-to-peer, manager-to-subordinate, or supervisor-to-manager. They can also exist between teams, departments, and divisions. They are too common in organizations, and smart leaders learn to manage them.

Take a look at the list below. Are any of these things happening where you work? These symptoms indicate there are relationship conflicts occurring in your organization:

- Employees stop communicating about business issues or withdraw from business conversations
- Employees don't return messages or e-mails
- Backstabbing or gossip is a regular occurrence
- Cliques exist
- Ideas are undermined
- Excessive absenteeism, tardiness, and/or sick days are occurring
- Lawsuits, grievances, or EEOC actions have been filed
- People love their work but hate coming to work

What happens if you don't address relationship conflicts in your organization? After all, it is easier not to. It's uncomfortable and takes time. Ray avoided dealing with conflict until it caused big problems for his company and his own career. Few organizations provide employees with the skills needed to deal with conflict effectively, and many managers and leaders do not model conflict management competencies. This can be very costly.

In fact, unmanaged employee conflict is perhaps the largest reducible cost in organizations today. It is estimated that more than 65 percent of performance problems result from strained relationships between employees—not from lack of skills or motivation. And these relationship issues occur at all levels.

To calculate the cost of conflict in your organization, contact me for a free Cost of Conflict Measurement Instrument. You will be surprised at the high cost of conflict. A few of these factors are identified below.

Cost of Unmanaged Employee Conflict

Wasted time

Think of a conflict with which you are familiar. How much time is spent either in conflict or talking about the conflict by the individuals involved? A few hours a week can add up quickly when conflict goes unresolved.

One government agency I consulted with had a long history of labor/management conflicts. The conflicts were not bargaining issues, they were relationship issues. And the costs of the conflicts were into the millions of dollars by the time they were resolved.

Another conflict in a twelve-person department had cost $32,000 in wasted time and lost productivity during the nine months the conflict lasted. And that was just one conflict out of many within the entire organization.

Too bad both organizations waited so long to take the right steps.

Reduced quality of decisions

When people cooperate and share information they make more effective decisions. Conversely, when information is withheld or distorted, any decision made cannot be the best one possible. Decisions made under conditions of conflict are always of lesser quality than decisions made when people cooperate.

One situation I mediated involved conflicts between a team of eight division heads. The issues were long-standing and deeply rooted with resentments, turf protection and power contests. Open hostility was evident between two of the people. Among the rest there was frustration and guarded communication. To make the best decisions for the organization, open communication and sharing of information was critical. Because of their lack of cooperation and withholding of information, poor decisions and organizational problems persisted. The hidden cost of those poor decisions was high.

Because this conflict had gone on for so long, resolution from within was no longer possible. I was brought in to act as mediator. At first there were raised voices, finger pointing and accusations thrown about. But eventually we came to a workable agreement. It was worth the time and effort because the vastly improved teamwork led to better decision making and execution. A side benefit was the morale and attitude boost among all of the employees who worked under these senior managers.

Loss of skilled employees

People go to work for organizations, but they quit because of people. According to exit interviews, chronic unresolved conflict is a major factor in more than 50 percent of voluntary terminations.

A small service business had excessive turnover due to the conflicts created by the way supervisors communicated and dealt with employees. They were being *bosses* instead of *leaders*. The company was getting a decent amount of business, but was struggling to be profitable because of the high cost of turnover. Once the leadership and conflict issues were addressed, turnover decreased and the company was more profitable without significantly increasing its volume of business.

What is the total cost?

The costs of unmanaged conflict can be surprisingly high. Smart leaders are waking up to the fact that they can no longer afford to ignore these costs. And the good news is that virtually all of them can be eliminated.

Six Smart Strategies to Manage Workplace Conflict

Here are six practical, concrete actions you can take to reduce the costs of conflict in your organization. If you are doing all of them you are most likely in good shape. If not, you may be headed for trouble.

1. Deal with workplace issues sooner rather than later.

Do you ignore conflict and just hope it goes go away?

You'll save time and be more effective by addressing employee conflicts as soon as they arise. Avoiding difficult conversations is detrimental to you and the organization. Most relationship conflicts do not go away on their own. They escalate into bigger problems. In fact, 80 percent of employee lawsuits and grievances can be prevented if proper action is taken in the early stages of the problem.

Think of a conflict with which you are familiar. What is the business problem created by the conflict? Examples of business problems might include wasted time, inefficiencies, missed deadlines, poor morale, etc. If the conflict goes unresolved, the business problems increase and become more expensive.

Resentments and bad feelings build over time. At best, unmanaged employee conflicts lead to unproductive behaviors and reluctance to work together. But the hidden risks and expense of lawsuits, grievances, EEO complaints, and workplace violence are even worse. And they are preventable.

2. Resolve conflicts at the lowest levels.

Do managers spend a lot of time dealing with conflict situations?

As conflicts rise up the organizational ladder, they become more costly and time-consuming. Conflicts are less destructive when the parties involved resolve the issues themselves.

Human resource executives tell me at least 75 percent of the employee issues that come to them should have been resolved and handled between the employees involved. As one put it, "I feel like I'm dealing with junior high or elementary school children. They run to us with complaints like we're the teachers who are supposed to 'fix' their problems." In many cases, otherwise smart, educated professionals simply don't have the skills to manage conflict.

When employees have issues with their co-workers or supervisor, or when a supervisor has an issue with a subordinate, the people involved need to have an adult-to-adult business conversation about the business problem. Most all conflicts can be resolved between the people involved without management intervention or kicking it up to Human Resources or union representatives.

3. Develop competencies in interest-based conflict resolution.

Do employees in your organization know how to approach and resolve conflicts?

There are only three ways to resolve conflict: using power, determining rights, or reconciling interests. The power method uses authority or position to dictate or coerce outcomes. The rights method uses rules, contract, or litigation to determine whose rights are more important than the other's. Interest-based resolution uses a process of identifying the underlying interests of those in conflict and determining options for meeting the interests of both sides.

The power and rights approaches always produce a winner and a loser. An interest-based approach is the only one where everybody can win. Interest reconciliation is by far the best method for a lasting resolution and is the most sophisticated form of conflict management. It encourages fairness, and when employees are able to disagree and confront conflict situations without retaliation, they develop open communication and trust. This leads to better teamwork and accomplishment.

Interest-based conflict resolution training is essential for all employees at all levels. It's easy to tell people to "work it out." But that can't happen when people don't know how to resolve their issues. In fact, most people do not know how to go about having the difficult conversations that are needed to resolve differences. The organizations that provide this skill-development training have seen significant improvements in productivity and profitability.

At a minimum, employees and managers need to know the basics of how to have a problem-solving meeting. Knowledge, skill and ability to use interest-based conflict-resolution skills are important. Here are the steps:

- Define and agree on the business problem
- Separate the people from the problem
- Determine everyone's positions (their stance or demand)
- Determine everyone's interests (underlying reasons for their positions)
- Brainstorm options for mutual gain (ways that interests can be satisfied)
- Build an action plan
- Follow up and reassess

I once consulted with a company that had a group of engineers who were mired in personality clashes and disagreements. These were educated people who wouldn't even communicate civilly within their team. They used power and rights contests to get their way or retaliate against each other. Resentments and animosities were deep. One of the engineers even spent a couple of hours a day documenting what everyone else was doing and how they were doing it wrong. It was a colossal waste of high salaries. Their manager had many failed attempts at resolving the conflict.

I used an interest-based conflict resolution approach with them. Each one believed that everyone else was the problem, and of course, they had lots of reasons and justifications for their positions. We defined the business problem and they agreed it was wasted time and poor departmental output. They also agreed they needed to resolve that problem. We explored the underlying interests and found many to be in common, including the need to be respected, professional integrity, management approval, job security, and mission accomplishment. For the first time, they started to listen and understand each other's point of view. This led to the breakthrough of changing from "me against you" to "us against the problem." They brainstormed options to resolve their issues and came to mutually agreed-upon rules for future working relationships. They also established a process to follow up with their agreement to avoid backsliding.

After learning and applying interest-based conflict resolution skills, they now know how to resolve future conflicts. All of the time and energy that had previously gone into their interpersonal conflicts is now directed toward accomplishing their mission.

The cost of providing training is miniscule compared to the cost of unmanaged conflict. To address issues at the lowest levels, all employees, especially supervisors, need to know core skills in interest-based conflict resolution. In addition, managers need to have competencies to resolve disputes between their team members for the times when employees can't work it out themselves.

4. Make agreements that "stick."

Do people keep returning to old problem behaviors?

Most of us have seen it happen. People come to a resolution only to backslide. It doesn't have to work that way. We just need to make sure we end up with agreements that will stick.

The goal of addressing the conflict is not to *punish, affix blame* or *get even* for past actions. Instead, it is to define how we are going to work together in the future in ways that satisfy the most important interests of everyone involved in the conflict.

I mediated a conflict between two government attorneys who had long-standing unresolved issues that had led to a very unpleasant work environment in their office. They finally came to an agreement that met the needs and interests of both. They felt optimistic about their agreement and anticipated working better together. They were all smiles and good feelings…for a while. The problem? They slid back into old patterns of behavior because they didn't follow up on their agreement. They should have had a smart agreement.

A smart agreement is one that is behaviorally specific, balanced, and in writing. There also needs to be follow-up. The parties need to get together after a period of time to trouble-shoot their agreement, see how it's working, and determine if there is anything else that needs to be included that was not thought of in the initial meeting. With a good written agreement and follow-up, backsliding will rarely occur. This is the step the attorneys failed to take.

5. **Remove obstacles that prevent people from effectively managing conflicts.**

   Do employees avoid confronting conflicts because they are afraid to "rock the boat?"

   Make it safe for employees to meet and resolve their conflicts. Make sure there is no sense of retaliation or of being punished for bringing up concerns in a tactful, professional way. When you are the one the employee has the conflict with, he or she should feel safe when meeting with you to resolve the problem. Remain calm and listen. Avoid being argumentative or defensive. If you don't, your people will stop coming to you or trying to manage their own conflicts appropriately.

Remember, when confronting conflicts, people are having a business meeting about a business problem. It is not personal and should not be taken that way. The goal is to work together more effectively in the future. When you are unavailable or unapproachable, the conflicts become buried and the hidden undercurrents and resentments grow and fester.

Here are some organizational "shoulds" and "should nots": Employees *should* be encouraged and supported to meet and work out their issues. The process *should not* be seen as taking time away from work. It *should* be accepted as an integral part of doing business. The norms and culture *should* be to resolve issues at the lowest level. It *should* be abnormal to not confront and resolve conflicts. Issues that escalate to grievances and lawsuits *should* be ancient history.

6. Model effective conflict management behaviors in your own day-to-day interactions.

Do the people at the top model effective conflict resolution skills?

Some managers abdicate their responsibility to develop people. They send employees to training classes and then expect them to change and apply new skills. In many cases, the employee doesn't see the manager using the skills the employee just learned, so the new skills are not reinforced.

Model the behaviors you expect from others. If you avoid dealing with conflict or shy away from uncomfortable conversations, the people under you will do the same. Before your people change, they first have to see your willingness to change. People will test you. Ultimately they do what you do, not what you say you do. If you tell people to work out their conflicts and they have conflict resolution competencies, then they can resolve their own issues. But it is likely they will do this only if they see you doing it, too.

Use effective conflict resolution competencies in your own dealings with colleagues, bosses, and subordinates. Make it a habit to define the business problems created by conflicts and focus on joint resolutions that solve the problem and that satisfy the interests of all parties involved. Your behavior will communicate your expectations much louder than words.

Encourage and expect employees to use their conflict resolution skills. However, there may be times when you need to step in and mediate conflicts between others. For example, while employees are in the process of learning how to resolve their issues, they may need some help and the added security of having assistance. Act as a neutral third party. Avoid the temptation to solve the problem for them or dictate a solution. The former creates dependency and the latter creates resentment. They need to come to their own agreement. You are there to facilitate the conversation between them and support their agreement.

Make It Happen

Ray applied these six strategies and is no longer stuck in his career. Within a year he turned things around. The payoff? He is now perceived as an effective manager and a good leader. Productivity is up and he has a high-performing, conflict-free department with great communication and teamwork. Grievances and complaints to Human Resources no longer come from his people and he has the lowest turnover and absenteeism rate in the company. He was recently selected for a promotion and was asked to be a key sponsor of a companywide conflict management task force.

The ability to manage workplace conflict is a core competency for every effective leader. You can develop this competency and lead others to develop it, too. And that makes you a smart leader.

CHAPTER TWO

Power Writing for Executives

A simple process that gets results!

Jonathan Clark

Jonathan Clark, owner of Scottsdale Seminars, Inc., teaches *Business Writing Solutions*. Organizations such as Southwest Airlines, NASA-Kennedy Space Center, RadioShack and the U.S. Postal Service regularly schedule his program. He has become a highly sought trainer in the federal government inspector general community.

Jonathan was a frustrated athlete. At 14, he had a choice between another year on the bench of his summer baseball team or writing articles on a local basketball camp for $2.00 per day. He retired from competitive sports to become a sports writer. His career path landed him with the NCAA.

But Jonathan loved to speak as well as write, so he left the corporate world in 1977. Since 1982 he has presented over 2,200 days of training all over North America. He wrote two books on time and priority management. When he started Scottsdale Seminars in 1996, he focused on business writing. He recently produced a CD-ROM version of *Business Writing Solutions* for self-study and review.

Participants love Jonathan's classes which are full of humor, fun and practical ideas. They tell him: *"I never imagined I would enjoy a writing class, but you made the subject come alive for me!"*

You'll find his chapter on powerful business writing educational and entertaining. Jonathan promises to teach you to write at least 30 percent faster than you do now!

Married to Susan since 1972, Jonathan lives in Phoenix with two Scottish Fold cats, Malcolm and Macduff. Jonathan has seen major league baseball games in 52 stadiums and attended over 200 different operas in 10 countries.

Scottsdale Seminars, Inc.
Phoenix, AZ • 877-398-5456 • www.scottsdaleseminars.com

Jonathan Clark

Power Writing for Executives

A simple process that gets results!

For a lawyer, he writes pretty well.

Herb Kelleher, the legendary founder of Southwest Airlines, rarely handled customer complaints since he had a staff of executive office writers who did that for him.

Every so often, a situation required his finesse and superior writing skills. This was one of those cases.

A regular flyer on Southwest had concerns—about nearly everything. The lack of reserved seats on the flight. The frequent flyer program. The peanuts. Standing in line waiting to board the plane. Flight attendants who sang songs and played games. She was not happy.

Several experienced writers took their best shots. No one was successful. The growing pile of communication landed on Kelleher's desk. He penned the final letter.

This series of letters owns a prominent display location in the hallways of Southwest's headquarters building at Love Field in Dallas. During one of my business writing training classes for Southwest, I scouted out the display.

This was my Holy Grail. I stood, transfixed, and didn't move until I had committed the entire letter to memory. I relive that memory, and the letter, in every class.

"Dear Ms. _____: We will miss you. Sincerely, Herb Kelleher"

This letter includes all the features of great writing. It was short. It was clear. It was personal. Most importantly, it worked. The customer got the message, stopped complaining, and still flies Southwest.

Powerful writing skills can transport you to the position you want in your organization, no matter where your career path leads or how high you rise. Writing skills can make or break your career. They are far more powerful than your business card or that face-to-face first impression.

Unfortunately, many business executives-to-be embrace a writing style that fails to communicate the image they want to portray. We write to *impress* rather than to *express*. We adopt every big word we can, construct complex sentences, bury our main ideas in long paragraphs, and write three pages to say what we could have said in one page.

Don't buy it! The best writers write clearly and concisely. It works for Herb Kelleher. It works for me. It will work for you.

I will make the writing process simple for you. I want your writing to be as natural as conversation, and I want you to enjoy it. I want it to succeed, and I want you to spend a lot less time working on it than you do now. I can help you write 30 percent faster. You have other ways to invest your time as you climb the organizational ladder.

Refill your coffee cup, grab the highlighter and get comfortable. I want to share these ideas with you!

First, recognize writing as a six-step *process*:

1. Preparing: Getting ready to write
2. Clustering: Generating ideas
3. Organizing: Structuring your cluster
4. Freewriting: Writing as much as you can as fast as you can
5. Editing: Fixing grammar, tone, flow and accuracy
6. Proofreading: Checking for typos and other stuff you don't want

Take these steps each time you write, take them in *sequence*, and keep them *separate* from one another. You'll learn why!

1. Preparing: Getting ready to write.

Learn the most important question about writing: Does it work? All business writing has a purpose: to inform, to document, to instruct, or to persuade. All that truly matters is did your writing accomplish its purpose? Did it inform? Document? Instruct? Persuade? If it doesn't work, who cares how much flowery language you used or how you might have impressed your high school English teacher? Focus from beginning to end on producing writing that *works*.

Think about your reader. Ask questions to focus your thoughts. To whom am I writing? What do I want to say? What action do I want my reader to take?

Don't let yourself off easily. You're thinking, of course, I should ask these questions before I write. *Do you?* Don't you get written documents every day that have failed to ask, or answer, these essential questions? You read it, you put it down. You say, I don't know why I received this. I don't know what I'm supposed to do now. Think the questions through specifically and answer them completely before you write.

Take the "business card" test. Write your main idea on the back of a business card. In *normal*-sized writing. If you can, you will write a powerful, focused message that *works* every time.

Picture your reader, and write as if you were having a conversation. The best business writing is conversational. It reads like people *talking* to one another. When we speak, we use vivid verbs and concise language. We express our ideas naturally, because conversation is natural. Do you need to write a customer letter? Write as if you were speaking to that person. Writing a letter for your boss's signature? Imagine yourself *as* your boss, and speak to the reader.

Call your reader's face to mind. If you're writing to more than one person, pick a representative of the group and picture that person. If you don't know the person you're writing to, imagine someone you do know. You just sat down for a cup of coffee. You know this person well. You are friends. What will you say?

I disagree with writing teachers and trainers who tell participants "Write the way you talk." We would be in trouble if we did!

Levels of writing differ just as our levels of conversation differ. You use a different approach and a different tone if you're speaking with an important person. Now think about the people you work with every day, or the ten-year-old who lives in your house.

2. "Cluster" your ideas before you write.

Put your main topic in the center of a blank page, and circle it. Now, think about anything and everything that comes to mind as you think about that topic. Write each idea outside the circle, then circle it and connect it to your main circle.

Don't judge your ideas. There are no bad ideas, so just let them flow. Some ideas lead away from your main circle, out on a branch. Let them take you there; you'll find a great insight waiting. Some ideas may suggest another cluster in addition to the main one.

Don't set a time limit, but don't try to force things, either. When the ideas begin to run out, stop. You will still produce ideas as your subconscious works on the topic. Add them to the cluster when they come. When you're done, it could look something like this:

The circular process produces a draft without rigid structure, unlike an outline. (Remember all those rules?) Because we put the ideas in a circle, we have no priorities. If we put things in linear form, we begin to rank, judge and prioritize.

3. Organizing: Structuring your cluster.

Next, organize the ideas into a structure to follow when writing. Do an outline now or rank the items in order of priority or some other sequence. Separate idea generation from organization.

A bonus. How else can you use clustering? This process will help almost any time you need to pull thoughts and ideas together. Use it to:

- Solve a problem. Put your problem in the center of a circle and cluster everything you can think of related to the problem. Don't worry now about putting the items in columns as positives or negatives. Do that later.

- Plan a project. Remember those brainstorming sessions? Have each participant cluster ideas before the group work begins. You'll have more ideas, better ideas, and more participation.
- Evaluate someone or something. Whether it's making a tough decision or writing a performance evaluation of the person who drives you crazy, use clustering to put things clearly and objectively.
- Make a list. I'm a list person, but the word *list* conjures up linear form. Cluster what you need to do first, or the steps of a project, or the resources you have for that project. Make your list from the cluster.
- Clarify a goal. Take a broad, vague, fuzzy goal. A five-year career goal? Cluster it out. In minutes you'll have broken that fuzzy goal into a series of realistic objectives you must accomplish to achieve the goal. Cluster each objective, and now you have… steps.

4. Freewriting: Writing as much as you can as fast as you can.

Separate the writing and editing steps. Your brain has two sides. They're not actually *sides*, but *processes*: creation (right brain) and analysis (left brain). We don't do a good job analyzing if we're thinking creatively. We're equally bad at creating when we need to be analyzing.

The biggest mistake most writers make. We try to write and edit our material…at the same time. This habit has controlled our writing since grade school. We write something then try to make it better. Did I spell that word correctly? Do I need a comma? Does that word communicate the *tone* I want? What's that rule on *who* and *whom*?

Separating these steps of writing and editing will be the most liberating thing you do as a writer. It unleashes your power and creativity. It helps you write at least 30 percent faster than you do now.

I call it freewriting. Write as much as you can, as fast as you can. Don't worry about spelling, punctuation, or grammar. Leave those for editing. If you get stuck for a word, keep going. If you write the wrong word, mark it, but keep going and come back to it later. Use your keyboard for freewriting…as long as you're not a hunt-and-peck typist. Use pen and paper. Talk it out as dictation. You can talk at least four times faster than you write, and your words will come out more conversationally.

Disable your computer's spelling and grammar checking functions. Since most people write using a computer keyboard, this is an important suggestion. Get up *now* and do this. Don't get me started on how much stupid, wrong, bad advice I believe these functions give writers. The main reason to turn them off is to help you separate the writing and editing steps of the process. The last thing you want while you're creating is to see those reminders in red and green—the misspelled words and the grammar problems.

Since these processes come enabled when you buy word processing software, you may need to go into the Options menu to disable them. You can still use the features as separate steps when you've finished writing, as part of editing. Just don't believe everything they tell you. Check a grammar guide and dictionary for the "final word" on this subject.

While you're at it, start up another function after you've disabled the automatic checking—the "Readability Statistics" option. (I'll tell you why later.)

Look for exciting things as you freewrite. Once you've gotten your right brain engaged and turned it loose, look out! You'll experience creativity in your writing like you've never had before. You'll put emotion in your writing (you might take it out later, but this helps creativity). You'll get insights as you write that you would never have while writing and editing at the same time. Right brain activities tune you in to your subconscious much more easily. Be alert to it as you write.

5. Editing: Fixing your grammar, tone, flow and accuracy.

Finally, do the editing. I'll let you get the grammar stuff somewhere else. I want to talk about turning your words into powerful communication, the kind that WORKS!

Make your writing concise. We write twice as many words as we need! This habit goes back to those school essays that had to include a specified number of words. We couldn't write that many, so we started padding. Adjectives and adverbs. Needless phrases. Expanding our ideas from sentences to paragraphs. Repeating ourselves. We added no quality to our work, just quantity, to achieve that word count.

William Zinsser's classic book, *On Writing Well*, suggests we can eliminate half the words we write, as we often fill our documents with words that do no work. If an employee didn't work, you would fire that person. We need to fire the words that don't help us communicate our message.

Needless phrases: *Someone has said that... You will want to know that... Please be advised that... I would like to tell you that...* Use these when you freewrite if you like, because they can trigger ideas. But capitalize the first word after *that* when you edit. Like the booster rocket on a space shuttle, it gets you launched, but you don't need to keep it.

"Smothered" verbs: "Performed an evaluation of..." means you *evaluated.* "Did an analysis of..." means you *analyzed.* "Held a meeting with..." means you *met.* "Made a decision..." means you *decided.*

Passive voice: Business writers *love* passive voice (making your subject the *receiver* instead of the *giver* of the action), but it weakens your message and adds extra words.

Grammar checking software does a decent job of identifying passive voice. Don't you wish it would tell you *how* you ended up writing passively? Or show you how to express your sentence in active voice, instead of the generic illustration it uses? It's not likely to do that soon. Look for these three clues:

1. The "action agent" at the end of the sentence: *The book was picked up by the **girl**.* The book doesn't do anything (it's passive); the girl does. But you have to read to the end of the sentence to find her.
2. A form of the verb *to be*: *A decision **was** made by the committee.*
3. The word ***by*** following a verb: *The checks have been signed **by** the treasurer.* If you could add ***by*** after the verb, it's also passive. *The checks have been signed.* They were signed ***by*** someone who remains unidentified.

To change passive voice to active:

1. Move the action agent to the beginning of the sentence: *The **girl** picked up the book.*
2. Don't use ***to be**: The committee **decided**.* I just reduced a seven-word sentence to three words by changing passive voice to active voice.
3. Follow the old sentence construction formula: ***Who** did **what** to **whom** (or to **what**). (**Who**?) The treasurer (did **What**?) signed (to **What**?) the checks.*

You may *choose* to use passive voice. Sometimes you want a slightly weaker message. Or, you may not know *who* did something, only that something happened. Perhaps *who* did it is less important than what happened. Be careful not to overuse this structure because it saps the energy and conciseness from your writing.

Don't use a big word when a small word will do. *Use*, not *utilize. Said,* not *stated. End,* not *terminate. Ask,* not *request.* Your document contains enough big words with technical terms and jargon. Connect them with short, simple, familiar words—the ones we have known all our lives. Ninety percent of communication in English uses just 2,000 words.

Write shorter sentences and use shorter paragraphs. I suggest 10-17 words per sentence, and 5-7 lines per paragraph. Don't let your paragraphs exceed 10 lines. Break them into shorter paragraphs.

Read your writing aloud, and listen. Your ear will recognize grammar problems, tone problems (wrong choice of words), and conversational writing.

6. Proofreading: Checking for typos and other stuff you don't want.

Don't confuse this step with editing. Print out the document to proofread it. Make it look as different as you can from the text you've wrestled with throughout the editing process. Change the typeface or the size or the color. You're much too familiar with what you wrote and edited—or you *think* you are. The disruptions help you see the material in a fresh way, as if you just sat down to read someone else's document.

Finally, thoughts about readability.

Remember activating the readability figures feature on your spelling and grammar checking? This feature provides information directing you to better writing.

Most versions of this utility list the total number of words, the average sentence length and the percentage of sentences you wrote in passive voice.

This will give you readability figures. You will also get a reading ease score based on a scale of 0 to 100. The higher the score, the more *readable* your document. Then you'll get a grade level based on the Flesch-Kincaid scale. The higher the grade the more *difficult* your document is to read. To improve the numbers, write shorter sentences, write conversationally, and use active voice.

The grade level is deceptive. If you score 12.0 (the top score on the scale), a person with a high school degree will be at maximum reading ability trying to read your writing. You can expect that person to comprehend perhaps half of your message. Try to attain an 8.0 or lower rating to maximize your writing effectiveness and reach your intended audience.

I just checked what I wrote in this chapter and came up with 10.2 words per sentence, 2 percent passive voice, a reading ease of 66.3, and a grade level of 6.5. This is a chapter almost anyone can read!

A few parting words of encouragement.

I hope these ideas jump-start your writing and help you write faster, with more success and more confidence than before. And please don't fall for the idea that long, complex writing is the key to success. I'll end by quoting William Zinsser:

> *Plain talk will not be easily achieved in business and government. Too much vanity is on the line. Executives and managers at every level are prisoners to the notion that a simple style reflects a simple mind. Actually, a simple style is the result of hard work and hard thinking. A muddled style reflects a muddled thinker, or a person too dumb or too lazy to organize thoughts.*

Practice Your Freewriting

Write as much as you can, as fast as you can.
Don't worry about spelling, punctuation, or grammar.

CHAPTER THREE

War and Sport

Office politics for women and the men who supervise them

Ann E. Mah, M.S.

Ann Mah, owner of Discover! Strategies and Compass Series Publishing, works with organizations across the nation on business and life strategies. Her thought-provoking and practical approach gives participants ideas they can use immediately. Topics most requested are men and women at work, presentation skills, leadership, business etiquette, networking, team building and developing a winning personal style.

A past national president of the American Business Women's Association, Ann knows the issues that matter most to successful executives. She brings the teaching style of a seasoned educator and over 20 years of corporate management experience to her seminars. Ann connects to her audiences through personal stories and a fun approach to learning. She provides customized workshops and keynotes for companies and conventions. Ann holds a master's degree in education and serves in the Kansas Legislature as a State Representative.

Discover! Strategies
Topeka, KS • 785-266-9434 • www.annmah.com

Ann E. Mah, M.S.

War and Sport

Office politics for women and the men who supervise them

It's been said that business is a combination of war and sport. Women don't get as much experience as men in either pursuit and we often take ourselves out of the game just doing what comes naturally. If you are a woman struggling to break through the glass ceiling, feeling as if you're on the outside looking in, this chapter is for you. Learn what every successful executive knows and how to make it work in your favor.

If you're a man supervising a bright, energetic woman who is executive material, but makes you crazy with her inability to *get it*, this chapter is for you, too. Why should you care? Simply put, corporate America can no longer rely on the available supply of men to manage its business. All human capital must be valued, and women are leaving corporate life in droves. They are unhappy, unchallenged, and under-compensated. When they've had enough, they take your training, your trade secrets and their contacts and either go to work for one of your competitors or become one of your competitors. Pay attention to the tips in this chapter, share them with your female subordinates, and help keep the brightest and best in your organization.

Office politics conjures up negative overtones, but we'll examine the positive side here. Office politics is the set of unwritten rules that determines whose ideas are heard and whose are not. Who gets promoted and who gets passed over. Who wins and who loses. You don't have to be a victim! You can use office politics to your advantage. An office politician is one who knows how to use personal influence to get things done, is sensitive to others' needs, and understands the corporate culture—and that's a good thing! Let's get started.

Your career connection

Bosses. Can't live with them. Can't live without them. Your boss is your first line of defense and your first connection to a promotion. A boss can make or break your career. I have to admit if there was a mistake to be made dealing with a boss, I probably made it. Fortunately, I had good mentors along the way, too. Here are some tips to help you maximize your career connection.

In business, the rules of engagement are not based on chivalry. Your boss is not there to take care of you and get you promoted. The rules are based on the military code of loyalty and winning. Further, the business world is not flat. Men understand better than women that we work in a hierarchy. Someone is always above you on the ladder. If you play your cards right, they'll pull you up.

When you get a new boss, get to know him or her. Find out what your boss's interests are both personally and professionally. Ask what you can do to help him or her get oriented. Your boss also will appreciate knowing the unwritten rules of the organization. You can soon be the "go to" person and a valuable part of your boss's team. Later, when you have an idea to sell, it certainly helps if your boss supports it—and you. Making that personal connection first is your ace in the hole.

If you work for a man, there are special considerations. For example, be careful venting to a male boss. Why? When you are venting to a male boss, he will usually think you want him to *fix* the problem when you simply want to be heard. Men like to fix things. So while you're venting, make sure that you let him know you don't need an answer, you're just looking for an ear. Better yet, save any venting for your women friends at coffee break. They'll understand.

The number one thing you can do to make your boss happy is to do your job well. Business is about solutions. When you have a *real* problem to discuss with your boss, be ready to offer a solution. Be respectful of your boss's time. It is okay to ask for advice once, but don't ask the same question twice. Also, don't ask questions to which you already know the answer. You want to be your boss's right-hand woman, not a problem child.

Also, don't forget that promotions are a two-way street. We expect our bosses to go to bat for us, but how many of us are working to get our bosses a promotion? Ask your boss what you can do to help him or her get ahead in the organization. Offer to take the lead on a new project or research a proposal in which your boss is interested. Your boss's success will become your success.

Finally, give your boss feedback that relates to results, not feelings. This is tough for women, because we take our relationships personally. When things are going badly with a co-worker, we like to share that information—with everyone. Personal conflict saps energy from your performance and adds no value for the company. Invariably, when asked what we think of someone at work, we talk about feelings. "I like her" or "He's a jerk" might be a common response. Bosses, especially men bosses, don't want to hear that kind of feedback. "He does his job well" or "Her team failed to make the deadline" are comments that deal with results and not feelings or personalities. Keep your comments on a professional level and you'll be asked for your opinion more often.

If you have a psychopath boss, or one who is not interested in helping anyone up the ladder, resist the temptation to go above his or her head. You'll get a reputation that will not be helpful. Just wait it out or transfer out. Most bosses are reasonable people who are striving for the same things as you. Make your boss a key career connection by working toward your mutual success.

Getting it done

You may have been to networking seminars, but do you know how to apply networking skills to internal company customers? A network is simply a set of mutual obligations. You scratch my back and I'll scratch yours. A drawback for women is that we are good at asking for favors, but far less adept at returning them. Learn to trade favors in the form of support and results.

Start building your internal network by offering to do something for someone who needs help. Do this without being asked. Find someone in your work group (even better if it's someone in another department) who needs a hand on a project. Later, expect to get the favor returned. The more favors you build up, the larger your network of obligations. When it's your turn to make things happen, you will have friends to call on. This shows your boss you know how to leverage your personal power—a trait of every successful executive.

Expand your internal network by getting to know those in the company at least two levels above you. Hard work and technical expertise will only get you to the lower levels of management. After that, promotions are based on who knows your name and abilities. Your boss can put in a good word for you, and that's a start, but those two levels or more above you will make the real promotion decisions. How do you get to know these key decision makers?

If your boss is one who is well connected and you are in a partnership with your boss to work on your mutual advancement (as discussed above), then ask your boss for introductions and opportunities to be in meetings with key players. Find out what community organizations upper level managers are involved in and get involved. When the annual United Way drive starts, offer to head up the campaign committee. Show the higher-ups that you know how to bring in the money. This is especially important if you are currently in a job that does not directly contribute to the bottom line (i.e., human relations or staff manager). You can show your ability to network and meet revenue goals at the same time. Also, when you make a name for yourself in the community, you are more marketable inside your company. Company executives understand how important it is to be good a corporate citizen.

Attend company events to show you are a team player. Even if you don't like golf, learn to play or you'll be out of the loop. The golf course is the perfect place to make the personal connections that carry over to 9-to-5 successes. When you decide to forego company outings, you forego the contacts that matter later when promotion decisions are made. Make your *net work* more effectively by expanding your personal influence and increasing your exposure to the people who make decisions affecting your career path.

Managing meetings

Let's say you have a great idea that will save your company time and money. You can't wait for the next staff meeting to tell everyone about it. At the meeting, the idea falls flat. You cannot get other team members to buy into it at all. What happened? You might be a victim of office politics.

Remember that surprises are for birthdays, not bosses! If you have a new idea to present, do not bring it up for the first time in a meeting without having advised your boss in advance. This is especially true if the idea is controversial or involves a large expenditure. In business, meetings take place *before* the meeting, not during the meeting. Most meetings are for finalizing ideas and gaining consensus. Your boss can go a long way toward helping you gain consensus, helping you identify the holes in your plan, or warning you that your idea is doomed before it is presented.

Know beforehand your opposition and your allies. Your boss might also help in that effort. Gather as much advance support as you can from your allies. Sometimes it is not the best idea but the best-packaged idea that gets the nod; so think about how you will sell your idea to each person in the meeting. Show how your idea will benefit both them and the company. Everyone wants to know "what's in it for me," so let them know. Selling your idea may require making some strategic trades. Getting people to move toward your ideas is a skill that can be learned. It requires compromise and finding mutual ground.

If you are in charge of a meeting, make the most of it by using tactical seating. Place your allies in between those who may oppose you and next to those who are undecided. If you are not in charge of the meeting, sit next to the person who is. Sit at the head of the table to show more authority, if authority is what you need. This is a helpful arrangement if you're giving directives or need more control of the meeting. For more openness and discussion, sit in the middle of one side of the table. Seat yourself so you have good eye contact with those you want to influence.

Get your signals straight with your boss if you are both to be in a meeting together. Know if you are expected to take the lead or just watch. When it is your turn to speak, be direct and get to the point. Don't let others interrupt you. Women are more likely than men to let others interrupt, so just ignore the interrupter and keep on talking. You can even hold up your palm toward the interrupter to indicate that you are not finished. Make powerful statements with specific points. If you have more than one point to make, say, "There are three reasons we should adopt the plan…." If it helps, write down a few notes so you don't ramble. Show that you have done your homework.

Finally, follow up afterwards to confirm commitments made during any meeting. Let those who gave support know that you will be there for them when needed. When you know and practice the art of meeting politics, you won't be a victim; you'll be calling the shots.

It's not personal…

Even though business is built on personal relationships, it's not personal; but women often take it that way. When you take things personally, it wastes your energy and keeps you out of the game. Here is how it started.

There are lots of wonderful things we learned as little girls at play and much has been written on that. Dr. Pat Heim, in her book *Hardball for Women*, explains that girls grow up in a female culture where we learn that everyone wins when we share and compromise. For the most part, we play one-on-one, usually with a best friend. When girls play games like dolls and house, Heim says, we share power. The purpose of our games is to develop relationships. Success is achieved when we all get along.

If you think back on your own childhood, I'm sure you'll agree. No one kept score. It was personal. "My doll can kick your doll's butt!" was something girls would not say, even in jest. As a result we learned to be good collaborators. What we didn't learn as well was how to play with people we don't like or who don't play by the same rules.

At the same time, little boys learned about sport and war. They usually played in larger groups. The goal of the game was always the same… to win! They learned that everyone brings something to the team. They learned that you can have fun, even with people you don't like. They also learned to leave their personal feelings on the field.

Now we're all grown up, and women, in many ways, are still playing the same games and we still don't know how to play with people we don't like. When we get clipped on the way to the goal line, we get mad and we stay that way. It's still personal for us, and that just doesn't work at work. When we focus on personalities instead of results, we become part of the problem and not part of the solution.

Guys are always keeping score and trying to figure out who's winning. They focus on winning the game, and that means results. Heim notes they use banter and teasing the same way they did as kids to throw the other side off balance.

A case in point. I was watching Oscar de la Hoya and Felix Trinidad go 12 rounds for the welterweight championship. Leading up to this fight there was a great deal of banter between the fighters, to say the least. Each one was trying to get the edge. They fought 12 hard rounds, and in the end de la Hoya asks Trinidad to go out for a steak. It was over. These guys had just pummeled each other and now they were going out to eat. Some women would see that as hypocritical, but it's not. It's just an acknowledgment that they finished their business and now it's time to move on.

I decided I needed to explore this gender difference issue because I had a situation at work where I got knocked down by another player in the game and I got mad and sulked about it. I thought that when my male co-worker tried to take my assignments behind my back, it was about me.

In truth, it had nothing to do with me. While I was getting mad, he was making points. Guess who was the big loser in that game!

What I forgot was that boys don't really care if you foul someone along the way, as long as you win. If you see the other team about to complete a pass, you commit a foul and take the 15-yard penalty instead. You're a hero. We actually reward boys quite handsomely for that kind of behavior while we're telling girls to play nice. I'm not talking about committing unethical behavior here. I'm just saying that girls often get hung up on rules and guys are looking for ways to win.

Sometimes the game turns ugly. Some players do believe in dirty tricks. Just remember that nothing other people do is about you. It's always about them. Even direct insults usually mean they don't like themselves. So don't buy into it. Know who you are and don't measure your worth by what others say. One caution though: Even when men are being friendly to you, they're trying to figure out how to get ahead of you. They are always keeping score!

If personal feelings are getting in the way of your success, try to separate the actions of your co-workers from your feelings about them. Instead of thinking about how much you don't like a particular co-worker, focus on using the strengths and talents that person brings to the team. Learn to use those strengths to get the job done. You'll not only be in the game, you'll reduce your stress level. That's a *very* good thing!

When the game is over, leave your personal feelings on the field. Be good to yourself and be a better team player at the same time. As a natural collaborator, you have valuable skills to bring to the team, too. Taking yourself out of the game is not an option.

Be a player

Business is like war and sport…and it can be fun and profitable for you. Make career connections, expand your internal network, make meetings work for you, and don't take business tactics personally. While there is much more to be learned, if you conquer these tactics you're well on your way to the executive suite.

Office Politics Personal Inventory

Start today to work on your political savvy. Prioritize the areas that need work and set a strategy to make improvements. Rate yourself on a scale of 1 to 5 (1 being "needs work," 3 "okay," and 5 "great") in the following areas:

	1	2	3	4	5	
1.						I support my boss after he/she has made a decision.
2.						I can count on my boss to recommend me to upper management.
3.						My boss turns to me to get things done.
4.						I know many people in other departments.
5.						I am active and well known in the community.
6.						Managers two levels above me know my name.
7.						I am invited to meetings with decision makers.
8.						People listen to me in meetings.
9.						My ideas are generally accepted in the company.
10.						I control my anger at work.
11.						I take constructive criticism well.
12.						I can work with anyone in my peer group.

Review your "needs work" areas and write down steps to make improvements.

Statements 1-3: If you are having trouble with your boss, write down the action you will take to improve this career connection.

Statements 4-6: If you need to expand your internal network, what steps will you take?

Statements 7-9: If your ideas are not being accepted in meetings, what will you do before the next one to be sure you are heard?

Statements 10-12: If you take things too personally, what can you do to stay on a more professional level?

CHAPTER FOUR

Careers in Motion – Hang on for the Ride!

Strategies for lifelong career self-management

Meg Montford

Meg Montford, Executive Career Coach and President of Abilities Enhanced®, guides individuals nationwide on creating strategies for improving their careers. Since 1986, she has motivated thousands to overcome tough career challenges, move up the career ladder and discover how to work their passions. Her success stems from trusting her clients to trust themselves.

"Believe in yourself and everything is possible!" is how Meg lives her life, grows her career, coaches individuals and teaches others. Her clients claim, "The kicker is her intuition. I think she had me figured out after our first phone call!" A graduate of two business coaching schools, she has not only learned *HOW* to coach, but to *BE* a coach.

Meg is a Master Certified Career Coach and Career Management Fellow. She is a contributor to a dozen nationally published books, frequently delivers group presentations, and is often sought by media for interviews on career-related topics. She promotes networking as key to career success by serving in leadership roles in career management and professional coaching associations. As an ExecuNet affiliate, she facilitates regional executive networking events. Meg is an adjunct instructor and mentor coach with Career Coach Institute.

Meg Montford
Kansas City, MO • 816-767-1196 • www.abilitiesenhanced.com

Meg Montford

Careers in Motion – Hang on for the Ride!

Strategies for lifelong career self-management

What is your career plan? You do have one, don't you? If not, listen up. Without a career plan you will not survive in today's world of work. Over the past few years many have fallen victim to the demise of the traditional employer-employee relationship. Layoffs critically impacted the U.S. workforce, with white-collar executives especially hard hit. Total job loss recovery is still a dream for those dropped off unemployment rolls after benefits ran out or who grabbed bridge jobs while waiting to return to professional careers.

Workplace topography continues to erode and reform. Take a look at the facts: Baby Boomers are retiring, outsourcing is the latest corporate cost-cutter, and technology is redefining job descriptions. Talent shortages are affecting select industries while outdated occupations propel ongoing layoffs. What can you do to protect your career—to safeguard your right to earn a living doing the work you choose?

Protection, per se, is not really an option since you have limited control when working for someone else. What you may *not* know is that strategic and proactive career self-management is possible and can give you some measure of control. Career self-management starts when you adopt career resiliency. This manifests into a state of mind that empowers you to control your own job satisfaction. Today self-reliance is the name of the new career game.

Shifting your reality into a self-reliant mentality requires a career plan—a roadmap that you create for your lifelong career journey. Realize that this plan will shift and flex as you move along your career path. You will encounter bumps in the road—events that will force you to adjust your course—but your map should stay intact. Following are six action steps for writing your own career plan. They will help you meet the requisites for a successful career: desirable, reasonable, and achievable.

Personal Branding

After working 20 years as an architect, Jack got caught in his firm's massive restructuring. He had been an architect for his entire life after college. Not always in love with his job, he had followed in his father's footsteps by attending his alma mater, went to work for the first company that offered him a position, and was still there—until the layoffs hit. The pay was comfortable, the people nice enough, and he didn't mind the commute. Never a go-getter, Jack had no problem doing his job. He didn't earn much special recognition, but his work was acceptable and his bosses considered him an "OK" guy. Jack was baffled and in shock by the news of the layoff. He didn't know what to do or where to turn. He felt shame and disbelief. All he wanted was to have his "safe" job back. He became engulfed in fear like he'd never known.

How would Jack's career have been different if he had structured it around his personal brand? Instead of proactively managing his career, Jack let his career manage him. He surrendered his personal power over his own career destiny. On the other hand, Sam took a different approach to managing his career.

Sam sat back with a smile on his face and reflected on his most recent job offer, Regional Vice President of Operations at one of his current company's major competitors. Not only was this a new job with a larger company, but it also brought a sizable salary increase and promotion. Sam hadn't been looking for this position—it found him. Since earning his MBA three years ago, recruiters had continually reached out to him. Sam was well known in his industry's networking circles as the one who got things done. He had a reputation for taking on the tough assignments and quickly turning them into profitable gains. In fact, his accomplishments had been spotlighted in various professional publications. He was considered an expert by media who requested interviews with him and then quoted him in their articles. He capitalized on his media connections by writing trade articles himself that were published in industry periodicals. Sam knew which career path he wanted to fol-

low, and he deliberately ensured that his success wouldn't depend upon his employment at any one company. He modeled his belief in creating his own job security

Just as smart companies create brand awareness for their products, workers must develop their own career brands. How do you accomplish this? Determine what makes you unique compared to others who are doing the same thing in your field. Then devise a campaign to market yourself to promote your talents and skills. Make this an ongoing career management strategy.

Much work goes into personal branding. How you create and cultivate your network is one of the most important variables. Don't think for a moment that networking is something you do only between jobs! Networking is so important that it rates its own action step—more about that later.

Visibility builds credibility. How well known are you for what you do? Presentation and publication are highly respected methods for increasing visibility. Get in front of your superiors, subordinates, and peers. Speak about what you know in order to showcase your expertise. Submit articles and white papers to industry publications to create personal brand awareness and build a solid reputation. Get recognition!

When your career is branded, you can take your talents and skills anywhere. In fact, they will be in demand. You will always be on the radar screen of smart recruiters who will seek you out when they have key positions to fill. You will be in the driver's seat making career choices instead of dodging road kill when your career is struck by layoffs. Through personal branding, you create your own job security.

Networking

Sue was the go-to person in both her financial services company and local community. Her name was always in the newspaper for leading a fundraiser, getting a promotion at work, or being a spokesperson for a worthy cause. Occasionally, her letters to the editor appeared in print, or her articles on retirement planning would be published. She genuinely liked people and enjoyed helping. Sue's neighbor was appreciative when she referred his son for a summer job at the construction company that her brother owned. To thank her, the neighbor introduced her to his uncle who had just sold his lake property for a 300% profit and was looking for the right retirement investment. Sue was thrilled to be able to help, and captured a sizable commission.

Is this how you manage your career? Building connections wherever you go? If you do, you can see how your network becomes an intricate web woven of all your contacts, actions, and intentions.

Networking is a lifelong, ongoing process with success measured by the key relationships that you build. It requires you to continually look for ways to connect people with other people—build those bridges! Staying involved through networking takes your career self-management to the highest level.

What you share speaks to your worth in the world of work. People will remember you more for what you give than what you take. When you are stingy with your knowledge or resources you imply that you place no value on other people. If you make it "all about them," you create a positive impression that enhances your brand and boosts your career.

There are many places and ways to network. Active participation in teams, committees, group projects, focus groups, networking events, professional associations, and more, puts the spotlight on your contributions. One way to identify networking opportunities is to regularly review the weekly business calendar in your local newspaper or business journal looking for appropriate events to attend. Another is to ask business colleagues and peers for referrals to events and groups that they find beneficial. A new way to network has entered the high-tech scene: online membership networking groups where you connect with people around the world.

Despite the importance of networking, some people find it challenging to actually do. They may lack the motivation, claim they lack time, or may not see long-range benefits derived from going to meetings and making connections. Unfortunately, they probably won't accept the value of networking until faced with a need that could have been met through ongoing networking.

Let's imagine the crisis of losing your job. At that time, you probably will feel lost and lack the confidence to start networking. What would finding a new job be like if you had only maintained an active, comprehensive networking database? If you wait until you lose your job to start networking, you've waited too long. Start today.

Assessment

Helen had been working for the same company for 25 years. Starting out as an office assistant, her company reimbursed her tuition so she could get her college degree in accounting. Shortly after earning her CPA, Helen progressed rapidly up the career ladder to department supervisor and then to vice president of finance. For more than two decades, though, Helen felt she was an imposter. She had "fallen into" finance, not having chosen her career but letting it choose her. Now, she was really tired of the field. Something nagged at her as if there were much more she should be doing with her life. But what could she do?

Can Helen start over? Or does she have to stay "stuck" in a field she doesn't find rewarding? Helen's first step is to figure out where her passion lies, then orchestrate her plan to get there. Almost anything is possible—no matter what your age.

If you are anticipating, desiring, or even fighting career change, assessment is the first step to achieving clarity. Assessments may be formal or informal, done alone or with a career coach. The important thing is to spend time in reflection analyzing your values, motivators, interests and skills. If you utilize formal instruments, complete two or three so you can compare and contrast results. Outcomes vary from instrument to instrument.

There are many kinds and brands of formal assessments on the market. One of the oldest and most respected tools is the Meyers Briggs Type Indicator (MBTI®). An assessment that measures your preferences in select areas, it can ultimately assist you in your personal and professional growth and development. The results can be applied to enhancing executive, organization, and/or team development, plus leadership, retention, conflict resolution, career management, interpersonal relationships, and more.

Another frequently used assessment in the workplace is the 360-degree analysis. Distributed and sold under many labels, this instrument measures how your peers, subordinates, and supervisor perceive you, and compares their perceptions to how you see yourself. When used appropriately, this tool can become a great launching pad for personal and professional growth.

A simple, self-administering tool is the DiSC® Profile. Your assessment results will clarify your behavior style in dealing with various personality types at work. It will tell you if you are an extrovert or introvert, people-oriented or task-oriented, and more. The results can help you improve your workplace interactions as well as your personal relationships.

Do you know what it would take to work your passion? If not, find out! Test your assumptions using assessments. Verify that what the assessments indicate is true for you. Once you know what really motivates your enthusiasm to work, develop an action plan to achieve your goals.

What if you already experience career satisfaction? You are lucky and ahead of the game! Assessments will keep you sharp and on your career advancement track. However, if your career is crumbling all around you—due to an ever-evolving workplace or disillusionment with your job—then a change is probably in order. Take time out to explore career alternatives that will filter more easily through your business reality.

Lifelong Learning

So, you thought you were finished when you got that MBA? Wrong! Though critical for meeting career qualifications, not all learning is achieved through formal education. We work in a "Knowledge Economy" where change occurs at warp speed. While company-sponsored seminars and adult education courses can contribute to professional growth and development, the only way to stay on top of the demands of learning is to take responsibility for your own training.

Books and periodicals are published every day of the week. Deciding what is important to read, and what is not, is a challenge in itself. Information overload can overwhelm the best of us. Can you learn to skim the important material and pass up the rest? Accept that reading is one of the most relevant activities you will ever do to maintain your career resiliency. Staying up-to-date on current events, knowing your industry's latest trends, and keeping your skills razor sharp will contribute to the overall value of your personal brand and ensure that you stay ahead of the learning curve.

"But I'm too busy to read!" I can hear you say. Listen to books on tape as you are driving or flying to business destinations. Use your computer to filter the key information and news you need each day. In fact, a cutting-edge technology called RSS (Really Simple Syndication) is making it even easier to get information delivered to your desktop by bypassing your email box altogether. Look for RSS feeds to revolutionize the way we all access our information in the not-too-distant future.

Communication

Communication drives business. Isn't that a powerful statement? Think about it. Every day we communicate with our colleagues, employees, teams, customers, vendors, families, and friends. How we communicate affects the outcome of what we do and what others do, too. It will add to or detract from our personal brand.

Communication styles vary from person to person. Most of us are predominantly visual, auditory, or kinesthetic in the way we express what we say and process what we hear. For example, in describing your positive reaction to a new idea, what are you more likely to say—the idea *looks good*, it *sounds great*, or it *feels right*? Once you know your style, you can flex it to communicate with others on a common ground using their style while appreciating their style differences.

A formal assessment can help you clarify your communication style. One such tool is The NLP Processing Order Survey™ developed by Linda Storey based on Neuro Linguistic Programming. The MBTI® mentioned earlier is another means by which your communication can be assessed.

Communicating to be understood is critical to building and sustaining relationships that will support your career success. It is important to listen and process communication from the vantage place of others. Put yourself in their shoes to appreciate not only what they say but also how they say it.

Life/Work Balance

Career resiliency and self-reliance complement each other to become one driving success force when you create life/work balance and commit to living it. That's one of the benefits of choosing to manage your own career—you can insert the element of balance. What is life/work balance? It is whatever *you* decide meets your needs. For some it means a 50-hour workweek, while for others it means 35 hours. For some it means 50% travel for work, for others it means being home every evening. Know what you need to keep your stress levels low and your productivity levels high. Job burnout results when you lack life/work balance.

Stress is one of the biggest barriers to life/work balance. Many studies have been conducted about the long-term effects of stress on workers. Stressors such as sustained overtime lead to hypertension and high blood pressure. On the other hand, giving employees more power to make their own decisions reduces their stress levels, as does letting them know that management supports them.

Decide how to create you own life/work balance. Vacations can clear cobwebs from your brain and recharge your work battery. If you are plagued by guilt whenever you go on vacation, or if you take your electronic gadgets with you to stay in touch with the office—STOP! Prolonged breaks from your job only work if you sever all ties. Wipe the docket clean and then focus on new and different things. It's OK to drop out of the rat race periodically. If you don't disconnect totally, your vacation will be wasted. Get your creativity juices flowing—take a break! You deserve it!

Working the Plan

How have you designed your career plan? Can you see that the six action steps blend together and affect each other? If not, choose just one thing to do to kick off your plan. What will it be? Join a professional association or subscribe to an executive magazine? It doesn't matter—just do something! Use the mini-assessment following this chapter to jump-start the process.

Become a change agent instead of a change resister to mold your own career. The only constant in this world is change. Making friends with it will brand you as a professional who wants to grow with the company instead of holding it—and you—back. And don't forget—your job security comes from within you. Take charge! Make it happen!

Six Easy Action Steps to Start Your Career Plan

Action Steps:

A. Personal Branding
B. Networking
C. Assessment
D. Lifelong Learning
E. Communication
F. Life/Work Balance

First, take a short quiz to recap the chapter. From the activity list below circle the letter of the action step each activity represents.

Second, choose at least two action steps to start immediately. (No fair choosing steps you already take!)

Third, create a spreadsheet to track all of your activity. Add one new action step each month. This document becomes your written career plan. Review it often. Revise as necessary.

Activities:

1. Subscribe to five business publications and read them regularly. What trends do you notice?

   A B C D E F

2. Join two professional associations and attend frequent events. Which peers do you want to establish long-term affiliations with? Why?

   A B C D E F

3. Write a professional white paper using your industry expertise. Where will you get it published?

   A B C D E F

4. Set up a weekly date with your spouse, partner or best friend. Where is your cell phone?

   A B C D E F

5. Buy the book, *Now Discover Your Strengths,* by Marcus Buckingham & Donald O. Clifton (The Gallup Organization, 2001). Using a code number in the book, do the online survey to discover your own strengths. What did you learn about yourself?

   A B C D E F

6. The next time you are in a group, listen closely to what is being said. Note the different words people use to discuss the same thing. How will this experience change the way you talk to these people in the future?

   A B C D E F

Answer key: (1) D, (2) B, (3) A, (4) F, (5) C & F, (6) E

CHAPTER FIVE

The Executive's Passport

Business etiquette for executives on the go

Jolene A. Savage

Social Graces…a lost art or The Gift of a Lifetime? is the message in every seminar that Jolene Savage presents. Jolene's God-given talent to reach and inspire individuals goes above and beyond expectation. She has been described as a passionate, fun-loving presenter who helps busy executives develop skills to enhance their personal civility to achieve personal and professional goals. Jolene combines practical skills with interactive, hands-on training and boundless energy, while providing the tools that build self-confidence and increase promotion potential.

As the founder of Social Graces – The Gift of a Lifetime, Jolene delivers effective, innovative instruction that exceeds participants' expectations. Not only has Jolene studied the fine arts on both the east and west coasts, she graduated from a renowned finishing Academy in Orange County, California. She also has over 30 years experience in sporting, equestrian, modeling, pageantry, coaching and speaking engagements as well as an extensive business background. Jolene incorporates her broad international travel knowledge into every spectrum of social, business and international etiquette.

Jolene's desire is for each client to improve and shape his or her personal development, providing the edge that will help them succeed in life and make life better for themselves and others around them. Jolene makes her home in Topeka, Kansas, along with her husband Scott and children Jordan, Landon and Mooréa Savage.

Social Graces – The Gift of a Lifetime
Topeka, KS • (785) 478-3364 • www.socialgraceks.com

Jolene A. Savage

The Executive's Passport

Business etiquette for executives on the go

Did you know... that the most popular business meal today is lunch? Are you aware that international trade is now, more than ever, on the express highway to business success? Before joining the ranks of the distinguished diner or traveling internationally, you may want to brush up on a few skills. This chapter will teach you how to make the most of the *power lunch* and how to be comfortable so you can focus on the business at hand. It will also help you get the *edge* you need at a time when every detail counts in today's business market. In other words, you want a million dollar experience rather than a dining disaster.

The Million $$$ Lunch

Scheduling the Power Lunch

When arranging a lunch date, remember there are two different kinds of business lunches. First, there is the lunch that on the surface appears to have a light, social, get to know each other feel. Its purpose is to establish a comfort level that sets the tone for future business relations. Second, there is the lunch where it is clear that business will be discussed. Business lunches are also used to evaluate a potential employee's dining mastery.

Scheduling a business lunch is actually quite simple. Once you have made the invitation, confirm the date. Be sure to make it clear when inviting your guest whether it is for business purposes or more of a social affair.

One way to make it clear that you are hosting the lunch is to select a location. "How about Linda's Cuisine? They have great ambiance." Repeat the details of date, time, location and a simple, "I look forward to seeing you then." Don't forget to arrange a place to meet such as the lobby.

> ***A business lunch should be scheduled three days to a week in advance. Give the guest a choice of restaurants and confirm the day before.***

The Meat and Potatoes

Lunch dates usually take place between 11:15 a.m. and 2 p.m. and can last on the average from one-and-a-half to three hours. Know how much time you expect the lunch to take and let your guest know. If you are the guest and have a time constraint, give your host that information.

When selecting a restaurant, several key aspects should be considered. The restaurant should fit the style of the person you are having lunch with. Keep in mind your guest's lifestyle, taste, culture, likes and dislikes. Know your guest's profile as well as you possibly can. Do not choose a destination the individual may be uncomfortable with—for example, too stuffy or too relaxed. When making your reservation, ask for accommodations away from doors and the kitchen to eliminate additional distractions.

> ***Make arrangements to have the bill and tip taken care of in advance. Always use a credit card, not cash.***

Most important, choose a restaurant that you frequent often. Your service will be better, your client will be impressed with the VIP treatment you receive from the staff, and the wait staff will be more willing to meet your needs. Always make reservations and express you are entertaining a very special guest. This will let the staff know you expect superb service.

Arriving

When hosting a lunch you should arrive first and wait in the lobby. If you must be seated before your guest, do not order anything to drink. First impressions are lasting impressions and you do not want a messy table greeting your guest.

> ***ALWAYS REMEMBER:***
> - ***To push chair in***
> - ***Tip maitre d'***
> - ***Send note of thanks for good service***

If you arrive late, simply apologize briefly and go on with the rest of the lunch. If your guest has a coat to check, simply do so, and allow your guest to precede you into the dining room. If you are the host you may suggest where you would like your guest to sit. When the guest arrives and the waiter asks for drink orders, ask your guest to order first. Ordering alcohol at lunch is perfectly acceptable. The rule, however, is to only order one.

> ***Sit opposite from your guest to provide good eye contact.***

If there is a large group and you order a bottle of wine, you should check for three things when the waiter or wine steward brings the bottle. First, check to be sure it is the wine you ordered. Then look at the cork to be sure it is moist and has been properly stored. Finally, taste the wine to see if it has soured. If the wine does not taste the way you thought it would (i.e., too dry), that is not a reason to send it back. You only send wine back if it has gone sour.

If there is a group and introductions are to be made, remember that in business "rank rules." You always say the name of the most important person first. If you are introducing a client to your boss, you would say something like, "Mr. Client, I'd like you to meet Ms. Boss." Then share a bit of information about something they have in common to start a conversation.

Ordering lunch should not be too tricky. Try to stay away from messy or difficult-to-eat foods. If you are the guest and are not sure what price range the host expects, ask your host for a suggestion as to what is good on the menu. If you are the host and are familiar with the menu, and with your client's tastes, feel free to make a few recommendations.

> ***Rolls: Offer to your left first, then pass to the right. Butter is placed on the bread plate first. Butter only a piece at a time.***

As the guest, be gracious and exercise the art of communication, such as a compliment about the restaurant selection. Always remain calm, cool and under control. Your only job is to conduct business and appear as you dine like this every day. Remember that the food is secondary to the business at hand. If you are the host, handle whatever situations come up, but don't make a scene. Don't call waiters over to the table if something is amiss.

When the time arrives for you to discuss business, usually after you have ordered the meal, the host rises to the occasion. Do not wait too long however, for the guest may become restless and you may not have time to finish the business matter. You may begin by saying... "Shall we talk about..." or "What do you think about..." Simple. Of course, the most polite thing you can do is to give your guest your complete attention. Cell phones and pagers should be on silent.

Caviar – Place small portion onto toast, add lemon juice and garnish of your choice. Lift toast to your mouth and take a bite.

Once the meal is finished, the host asks for the check. The host usually pays. If you are the guest, you can return the favor at a later date. Quickly look over the bill, figure out the tip (17-25%) and turn the check face down along with your form of payment. Never accept your guest's polite offering of leaving the tip. You may download a wallet-sized tip guide at www.socialgraceks.com.

Winding Up

As the end of the lunch approaches, always wait for the host to lay his or her napkin on the table first to signal the completion of the meal. If you are the host, never request the check before all diners have finished eating. Be certain to thank your host upon leaving and send a thank you note within a day or two.

Fried Chicken – Use knife and fork to remove meat away from the bone.

Only use hands to eat chicken when the host signals to do so.

There are many other basics not covered in this chapter that you should know. You can test your dining decorum with this short test. Answers are at the end of the chapter.

a.) When do you place your napkin in your lap?

b.) Before excusing yourself to the restroom, where do you place your napkin?

c.) Between bites what is the proper resting position for the utensils?

d.) To signal to the wait staff that you are finished, the utensils should be placed in which direction?

e.) What is the unspoken code to get your waiter's attention?

f.) Your utensil falls onto the floor; what do you do?

g.) What do you do if you spill food on your guest?

h.) You have something in your mouth that must come out. How do you get it out of your mouth?
i.) What do you do if you see your lunch companion has food on his or her face?

One Last Thought on Lunch

You may be at the top of your game, but with the growing trend toward business lunches and international trade, your boss should feel confident knowing you are equipped with the right etiquette to make his or her name and the company look good. This is a small example of the importance of etiquette and protocol in corporate America and around the world. Be certain you are well equipped for any situation you may find yourself in. If you plan international travel…read on.

An American Executive Abroad Is Very Noticeable: Lessen the Obvious

Quick Tips for Entertaining Foreign Guests

If you are a young executive beginning your career, or an executive climbing the corporate ladder, you may very well find yourself entertaining a client from another country. In this section you will find a few tips on how to handle international visitors with comfort and finesse.

1. Know some phrases in the language of your guest. You will look better in their eyes, and they tend to open up to you when you have made an attempt to learn their language.
2. If you are hosting a dinner party, provide your international guests with a menu and agenda in both the local language and in the guest's native language.
3. Never use profane language, crude jokes or stories in the company of an international visitor. He or she may be terribly offended.
4. Dining etiquette varies widely around the world. Be sure to know the dining rules of your guest's home country so that neither of you is put in an embarrassing or uncomfortable situation.

The most important thing for you to remember is to make a sincere and genuine effort to be flexible, gracious, respectful and kind. Business will transpire, agreements will be made, contracts will be signed, and profits will be realized.

Quick Tips for Traveling Abroad

If you are chosen to travel to a foreign country on business, equip yourself with the proper tools for a successful venture. Here are some quick tips for foreign travel.

1. Make certain an interpreter has been engaged for you in that country.
2. If you are unfamiliar with the language, have your business cards printed on the back in the language of the country you are visiting.
3. In America, positive eye contact is a must. Be sure to know the protocol of the country where you are traveling.
4. Help the interpreter by using short sentences. Always ask, "Did I explain it clearly?" "Are there any questions?"
5. Treat the interpreter with kindness.
6. If two officials of equal rank share an interpreter, the interpreter should be seated between them at the table.

Finding Information on Foreign Cultures

1. Ask a librarian to recommend a book on the country in question.
2. Ask your company officials for any instructions.
3. Call the embassy of that country in Washington, D.C., and ask to speak to the Cultural Attache or the secretary to the Ambassador.
4. Contact international tourist agencies.
5. Contact the Commerce Department in Washington, D.C.
6. Know how the country's government is structured.
7. Know the top leaders' names.
8. Know the national religion.
9. Learn about the dietary laws.
10. Know which day of the week is their day to rest, if applicable.
11. Know the national holidays.
12. Know names of the country's museums, cathedrals, temples, and leading universities.
13. Learn about the country's major agricultural products, leading exports and the country's local celebrities.

The more knowledgeable you are about the country you plan to visit, the less likely you are to offend its people.

General Advice

Learn to speak these 15 phrases in the country you plan to visit:

1. Hello
2. Goodbye
3. Please
4. Nice to meet you
5. I am sorry
6. The food is delicious
7. I am having a great time
8. Please come visit us
9. Thank you
10. No, thank you
11. I love your country
12. My company makes....
13. We are a very big company
14. That is very impressive
15. Help

Important Numbers:

1. Citizen's emergency center in the State Department, Washington, D.C., 202-647-5225
2. Government operator in Washington at 202-647-1512. Ask to be connected to the duty officer at citizen's emergency center.

Putting It All Together

It has been proven by etiquette experts that those who possess the skill of social grace have an edge in the arena of life. Learning good dining etiquette and international travel rules will give you the edge needed to succeed in an increasingly competitive business environment. Knowing the rules and using them shows your respect for yourself, your colleagues, and your business partners. In a time when every detail counts, be sure you know the Social Graces.

...How Did You Do?...

Answers to the dining decorum test.

a. Follow the lead of your host.

b. Place the napkin in your chair.

c. The proper resting position for the utensils is in an upside down "V" with the fork on the left (8 o'clock position) and the knife on the right (4 o'clock position). Knife blade in and fork tines down.

d. The proper position is to place both utensils across the center of the plate from 4 o'clock to 10 o'clock.

e. Use eye contact to signal your waiter. Never raise your hand or yell their name.

f. Leave it there until the end of the meal. You may pick it up when you rise to leave or let the waiter know.

g. If you spill food on your guest, offer to pay for the dry cleaning.

h. Food comes out the same way it went in. If you used your hands to eat the food, then you may use your hands to remove it. If you used a fork, then remove it with a fork.

i. You are doing your companion a favor by letting them know about any food on their face.

CHAPTER SIX

Get the Cow Off Your Desk and the Monkey Off Your Back

It's all about paper flow and time management

Valerie Simpson

Valerie Simpson is an expert at helping clients overcome the barriers that limit effective, efficient business success. Her chapter discusses solutions to your paper flow and time management challenges. She offers stories that you may relate to and lets you see yourself "in the solution."

Valerie has over twenty years experience in managing, organizing and coaching others. She is different from most professional organizers in that she and her staff coach people to draw out the knowledge they already possess and teach them how to create systems that work for them. They provide tools that are based on how the client operates. It's always a work together partnership. Valerie believes that the ability to "*Find Anything Within Seconds Using Creative, Efficient Solutions!*"™ is possible for everyone.

Valerie has appeared on television shows such as *Sonoran Living*, *Good Evening Arizona*, *News Channel 3* and *TV 15* organizing a workstation, office, and even a walk-in closet. She has been a guest on several radio talk shows including *Your House Is Your Home* on AM Radio 1100 in Phoenix, Arizona, sharing client experiences, her expertise and the benefits of using Organize-U services.

Valerie has been published in several national magazines and many local Arizona publications. Valerie is also the creator, editor and publisher of the monthly eZine *Organizing You*. Valerie loves roller coasters and the excitement in amusement parks. She also has a son and daughter-in-law living in Texas.

Valerie Simpson
Phoenix, AZ • 602-212-0857 • www.Organize-U.com

Valerie Simpson

Get the Cow Off Your Desk and the Monkey Off Your Back

It's all about paper flow and time management

Has something like this happened to you recently?

It's time for an important meeting. Or perhaps you've just received a phone call you've been wanting and expecting. There's a big business deal on the other end.

Your boss walks into your office and says "I need to see the Acme Report right away!"

You look at your desk, and you don't have a clue where anything might be. The agenda for the meeting. The letter and proposal that prompted the call. The report. All you can see is the Cow sitting there.

The Cow doesn't actually look like one, but it might as well. Your desk is covered with piles and piles of paper. You haven't seen the bottom of the pile for weeks. You know what you need is in there—somewhere. You heave a big sigh and start to dig away. The Cow looks at you and laughs.

At times like this, you're convinced of one thing: organization is important. It's important to your credibility, your performance, your promotion, and even your job security. They're all at stake, even when you eventually find what you're looking for.

I talk to people like this all the time. As a professional organizer, I get the 911 calls. My clients will put up with the Cow for a long time, and usually send out the distress signals only when the emergency arrives.

Stephen Covey discusses this situation in *First Things First.* He calls it the Tyranny of the Urgent. Keeping things organized has always been important, but it's not urgent. So we go on doing other things, ignoring (or trying to ignore) the ever-growing Cow occupying our work area.

Then the fateful moment arrives, and we need something—NOW!

You can wait until that moment, pick up the phone (when you find it), and call someone like me. Or you can take a few moments every day to eat that Cow, just a few bites at a time. Eventually it will disappear, if you start now and stick with it.

Let me show you how to do it. We'll deal with the Cow first, then look at ways to prevent it from coming back.

Consider what the Cow costs you in productivity

How much do you earn annually? $50,000? $100,000? $200,000? More? What do 15 minutes a day of lost productivity (the time you spend looking for things you should be able to reach instantly) cost? At $50,000, it costs more than $1,500 per year. Double that for $100,000. A $200,000 earner wastes more than $6,000 of that in the search process. That's a lot of waste. How could *you* spend that kind of instant raise?

First, make this commitment to yourself: you're going to invest those 15 minutes a day, every day, in deconstructing the Cow. Each day you spend at that will reduce the time you spend looking for things. When you're finished, the lost time drops to zero. Here's how.

One bite at a time

If you're going to eat your Cow, begin with a small bite. The first step requires some office supply inventory you'll need to gather together or buy. Banker/storage boxes. New file folders. Hanging folders. Markers. There is a detailed list of supplies at the end of the chapter, or *I'll make it even easier for you.* Go to my website, www.organize-u.com, and click on the "Shop" link. You can do all your shopping there and have the items shipped to you.

Sweep your office

Decide the most important place to start in reorganizing your office. The most important place is the area that gives you the most pain. Perhaps you have stacks and piles all over the right side of your desk that keep sliding onto your work area. This would be a great place to start. Just begin there and work your way around the room sorting and putting things where they belong using the OHIO system.

Many people are overwhelmed with the task and I suggest that you just set a timer for only 10-15 minutes. Don't take on too much at one time. Remember to take it "one bite at a time" and you will get it done. Congratulate yourself on the small steps you are taking.

Have you heard the term "OHIO" (not the state)? Well, that stands for "**O**nly **H**andle **I**t **O**nce." To accomplish this I recommend using the "D-FAT" system:

- **Delegate** – When you can have someone else do it. Let them do it!
- **File** – When the document belongs in your file, put it there (or in your out/file tray), and get it off your desk.
- **Act** – When you can complete a task in less than five minutes, do it now. Take that action, and get it off your desk.
- **Toss** – When you don't have any further use for it, throw it in the trash, shredder or recycle bin and get it off your desk (and out of your life).

The Cow turns into a pile

Gather all your papers and folders into a huge pile.

Assemble the boxes, but leave the lids off. Stand them up on end and label each one with a Post-It type of note: Current Business, Potential Projects, Creative Ideas, Personal, Marketing. You'll identify your own major topics and no doubt create others as you sort.

Now you have a goal: to handle only once each paper or file in the stack, and put it into the appropriate box. Lay the documents flat on the bottom of the box (it's open on the side, remember) and place them face down in the new stack. This process will prepare you for the next step of adding these items to your filing system.

Look at your filing system

What kind of files do you have? Do you have your most important files at eye level, where you can find them easily? Have you labeled them clearly, so you can see them the minute you open the drawer?

If the drawers open to show the files arranged horizontally (across) instead of vertically (front to back), are they facing a direction that allows you to reach into the file drawer with your right hand, if you're right-handed, or the left, if you're a lefty?

Do the "Simpson Shuffle"

This simple step I developed amazes my clients and works spectacularly for them! Most people take a new file folder out of the box, label it on the tab at the back, place it in the file and start filling it.

Have you had difficulty finding a folder because you couldn't read its label? Perhaps some oversized papers blocked the tab. Maybe you've just crammed too much in the folder.

Or, have you had difficulty locating the front of the folder? You see the back of it clearly, but all the paper in it makes you wonder, "Where's the front, so I can place my most current document there?"

Well, it's time to do the Simpson Shuffle. You'll need a good-sized black marking pen or label maker for this job, because you're going to re-label most of the folders in your drawer.

Take the entire folder out of the drawer and remove all the paper. Now, *invert* the folder, so the label tab sticks out at the front of the folder, instead of the back. You may have to re-label the folder on the new "front" side in your large black marking pen or label maker. Then put the papers back in the folder and return it to your file.

When adding new folders to the drawer, check to see which folder tab works best. When you place a folder between two others, one having a left tab and the other having a right tab, the new folder should have a center tab.

Now the label is at the front of the file. Nothing will block your view of it. And if you want to put something in the front of the folder, it's as simple as sliding the new document in just behind the front cover—now the most prominent feature of the folder.

The Simpson Shuffle is the major element in the Simpson Pull System. This is exactly the process I follow when I'm working with my clients.

The Rubik cube of colored folders

A word about folders: I would caution you about the use of colored folders. The mind sees the colors like we see a Rubik cube. It's helpful when they are sorted by category or department or company. It's not so helpful when there is no rhyme or reason.

Most clients that have file system challenges have too many colored folders in their drawers. Changing from colors to manila or only one color of folder changes the dynamics of how the brain processes the information in the file system.

The biggest challenge of systems that use multiple colors is that when the user runs out of a particular color they grab whatever is available. Solution: Use all single color folders, preferably manila. And when you must use color to signify a difference in category or department, use a colored highlighter and mark the manila folder across the top of the tab.

The only time I have utilized color folders was for a client who ran five companies out of one facility. The agreement was that there would be no co-mingling of file folder colors between companies.

Organize your file drawers

This is an ideal time to use boxed-bottomed hanging files when you have the ability to hang them. This allows for easier movement in the file drawers, and keeps anything from becoming so bulky you can't open the folder (or put something into it) without removing the entire file. There is a list at the end of my chapter for the kind of hanging file I recommend (several brands I absolutely do *not* recommend, because they're just not sturdy enough to endure).

Think about the best way to present your files to your (or someone else's) eye. Alphabetically? By area or topic? Chronologically? A combination?

As you rearrange the files, make sure each folder contains information you currently use or need. If not, remove it from the active drawer and put it in an archives drawer or just discard it. Make new folders as you identify a need for them. When a folder gets particularly large, just use the crease marks near the fold to create a boxed bottom folder or split the file and have two, making sure that they are both appropriately labeled. I also recommend that you only allow a file to get to be 1 ½ inches thick and no more.

Sort the banker box piles into the file drawers

Now that you have your files Shuffled, Hanging, Removed, Organized and Fixed, it's time to take your papers and piles and put them in the proper locations. You'll have them off your desk once and for all, and your Cow will be gone!

Keep the Cow from returning

Of course, it's easy for that belligerent bovine to climb back up on your desk. All you have to do is let the paper start to accumulate again, without handling it and moving it along. So at least once a week, take all the paper you have and file it again.

Time and motion experts say we handle a typical piece of paper eight to ten times before we finish dealing with it. The ultimate goal is to handle everything just once, but of course that's not always possible. When you ask the right question, you'll probably cut the number of times you handle paper in half. Your paper should *flow* across your desk.

In order to *flow*, it has to *move*. So here's the question to ask, each time you pick something up: "What can I do with this paper to keep it *flowing* across my desk?" You'll find a number of options spring to mind.

I recommend that you use the OHIO and D-FAT systems here. Remember to keep the paperwork flowing, always in motion.

You can also create a set of "active" desk files for the most critical things. I call this "*The Priority Folder System* (The solution to your Inbox nightmare)" They're brightly colored vinyl, guaranteed to last on the job as long as you do (even longer!), and you can create a system to make active files easily accessible.

I labeled them (on the front side, of course, using the Simpson Shuffle) **To File, To Do, Bills Due, Urgent, Pending** and **To Read.** You may create your own or purchase a set from my web site. They are vinyl, already labeled and built to last.

Keep these files in an easily accessible location. You may decide to put them in an incline desktop file rack on your desktop, or in the front of a nearby file drawer in a hanging folder. When something arrives on your desk, you have an easy system for prioritizing and then you just place it in the appropriate folder.

The durability of these folders makes them portable, too! If you're headed out to a meeting, or leaving town and going to the airport, grab the folders you need and put them in your briefcase. I particularly like taking the **To Read** file with me when I travel or go on appointments. Too often, we neglect the part of the job that requires us to stay informed and current.

How many times have you been waiting for someone or something and there you are reading a magazine that has no interest or value? Wouldn't it be nice to have your reading materials with you so that you can utilize that "down time" for something useful to you or your career?

Think about how paper moves across your desk

Did you know desks are right-handed or left-handed? So are we. When you play golf, you wouldn't dream of playing with the wrong kind of clubs. Yet we tolerate the same sort of awkwardness with our desks and flow patterns across them.

One of my clients owned a beautiful large desk from which he ran the business he owned. This desk was long enough to serve as the landing area on an aircraft carrier. It had graceful lines and a sweeping pattern toward an area for his computer and printer.

There was only one problem: the computer area (where he spent the most time) was off to the right and he was right-handed. That meant the entire surface area of his large desk was on his left side. When I explained it, he said, "No wonder I had a Black Hole for paper over on that side!" He now understood why the small area in front of the paper drawer for his printer always had a pile of documents in front of the drawer, making it necessary for him to pick it all up and move it to refill the paper drawer.

Maybe your desk isn't that spacious. Perhaps it is the standard rectangular shape, and maybe your computer equipment is off to the side (or behind you) on a credenza or shelf. You can still make your desk right-handed or left-handed. I'm going to describe what a right-handed person would do. If you're left-handed (as I am), you can simply reverse everything I say.

By the way, research shows that you can improve your productivity by as much as 50% by working in the correct left- or right-handed set-up.

Creating a paper flow

As you sit facing the work area in the middle of your desk, what do you see? Do you have an inbox? If so, it should be in the upper right hand corner of your desk.

From there, your paper can flow to the work area in the middle of your desk (you'll bring it there with the appropriate hand), where you can "execute" (love that word!) your work.

Once you've finished, it can go to your outbox, which you'll find in the upper right-hand corner just under your inbox. (Place your outbox items facedown. This will keep your eyes from wandering to what's completed. It will also make filing easier because you will file first things first.) What, you don't have an outbox? No wonder you have a Cow on your desk! Get one! (An outbox, that is.)

Some paper has no further use once you've "executed" it. So it goes into your wastebasket *off to your left*.

That's all there is to it. It's simple and easy to set up. Just think about paper flowing across your desk from right to left. And reverse the entire process if you're left-handed.

Pile trays

Don't even get me started on "pile trays." I found that having only two stacking trays on your desk works best: one on top for your inbox and one below that for outbox or "to file." Any more than that and they become pile trays that you will find yourself digging through just to find something.

Another way to do all this

I have many professional organizers with whom I'm affiliated. You may still want to hire an expert to help you do all this. One of my clients hired me because he knew he would never set aside time to do it himself, but when he brought me in, he would work with me as long as I was there. Perhaps you need that sort of incentive.

The Cow and the Monkey

So the Cow is gone, hopefully never to return. What about the Monkey? No, I haven't mentioned the Monkey yet.

The Monkey works along with the Cow. It jumps on your back and wraps its arms and legs around you. It looks over your shoulder, and whispers in your ear:

"You're the most disorganized person
in the world, aren't you?"

"You'll never be successful with a
mess of an office like yours."

"Why don't you do something about this?
That's just the way you are."

Once you've gotten yourself organized using these easy methods, the Monkey will sing a different song.

"Look at that Cow. Wait...where did it go?
Well, I guess I'll be going, too."

Good luck to you in your career, and may you find no Cow on your desk or Monkey on your back!

Shopping List...
List of recommended supplies to get you started

1) Lots of garbage bags
2) Economy Storage Boxes, 6/Pack
3) Pen-Style Highlighters, Assorted
4) Mini Metal Binder Clips, 9/16" size with 1/4" Capacity (use these instead of paper clips)
5) Staples Economy Manila File Folders, Legal or Letter, 1/3 Cut, 100/Box

   Please note that the File folders I listed are LEGAL or LETTER size. Please confirm you are ordering the correct supplies for your needs.
6) Pendaflex Ready-Tab Hanging File Folders, Legal or Letter, Standard Green, 25/Box

   **Please do not purchase the low-grade folders; they will fall apart and it's just not worth the frustration
7) 2" Pendaflex® Box-Bottom Hanging Files, Legal or Letter
8) Incline Desktop File Rack, Chrome, 8 Compartments

POWER TOOLS

SECTION II

Tools to Build Winning Teams

CHAPTER SEVEN

It's the People ...Stupid!

Inspire your employees for business success

Deb Clifford

Deb Clifford is an internationally recognized business leader who has spent the past twenty-one years working with organizations of all sizes building confident and capable leaders.

She is an accomplished keynote speaker and prominent learning advocate. Creator of the *Manager to Leader* ™ program used throughout New England, she brings her leadership and team development expertise and contagious enthusiasm to organizations. Her focus is to help build bench strength and drive strategy with the core group of people who create company results every day—the managers.

Ms. Clifford is the founder and CIO, Chief Inspiration Officer, of Inspired People. She brings her powerful message and successful programs to Fortune 500 companies, entrepreneurs, and associations. A member of the National Speakers Association and the International Federation of Speakers, her most requested seminars and keynotes provide strategies for inspirational work, life, team building, and change.

A recent attendee put it this way, "*Deb has walked the walk. She is one of the best presenters who ever graced the stage of our many conferences and seminars.*"

Learn to engage your people for business success with Deb's chapter on inspirational leadership. Get inspired!

Inspired People
Simsbury, CT • 1-860-217-4566 • www.inspiredpeople.com

Deb Clifford

It's the People ...Stupid!

Inspire your employees for business success

Many people don't love their work. They love to *hate* their work! Consider the popularity of the "Dilbert" cartoon series. I created a quick, inexpensive employee commitment survey (this took years of scientific research). Try it. Do a walk about your work area. Sample a few different departments—even a few different geographical locations if it applies. Count the number of "Dilbert" cartoons posted. Hmmmmm.

Now consider that you are depending on these people to meet your business goals. You are depending upon them to provide extraordinary customer service, extraordinary products, and extraordinary breakthrough technology. Yet, they have a cartoon focused on workplace absurdity and futility placed in front of their faces daily. They have a cartoon that portrays managers and leaders as buffoons. Inspiring, eh?

I am not against the cartoon. I simply make the point that it touches our people. They identify with the content. Why? Because all too often it reflects exactly how they feel ...uninspired.

Employees fall into the following four categories: inspired, tired, uninspired, or conspiring. In organizational development terms, this translates to engaged and disengaged. Employee commitment and engagement are the focus of many companies as they struggle to reach results and boost their profits through their *people*.

Inspired employees are engaged at work. They understand where the organization is going and the part they play in getting it there. They know their strengths and have a passion for sharing them. They have their priorities straight and make the necessary time to keep an equilibrium between vision and action.

Tired employees are tapped out. Their passion is lost somewhere in their burgeoning in-box. They are busy. Not focused, but busy. The lack of balance between their "to-do" list and the "why am I doing it" list has them running in circles sapping their energy all the more. As Stephen Covey said, their production capacity is drained, negatively impacting their actual production.

Uninspired employees are passively disengaged. Conspiring employees are actively disengaged. If an employee is actively disengaged, you know it. They are conspiring at the water cooler to get folks to join them in their dissatisfaction. They are in your face with their disengagement.

Then there are the passively disengaged. Whoa! Watch out—these are company culture killers, passion assassins, and bottom-line leeches. The uninspired are the walking dead of the workplace. They arrive and leave with little impact on the company vision or their fellow workers. They are just there.

When employees are tired or uninspired at work, everyone suffers. Studies show that the ratio of engaged workers to disengaged workers drives financial outcomes of organizations. In fact, only one in four employees is engaged at work, with 19% *actively disengaged.* The cost of disengagement is high, an estimated $350 billion in U.S. businesses alone.[1]

The relationship your organization has with employees can make or break the successful completion of plans and goals. Treating people right isn't just the right thing to do. It is one of the best things you can do to increase productivity and improve bottom-line results.

It is not about that two-page mission statement crafted at the last ten-day executive retreat. It is not about the clever strategic plan. It is not about the latest breakthrough technology. I had a light bulb moment the day I realized that, it's the people ...stupid! Do your people 'get it'? Do they believe and live your mission—your cause? Do your people feel a part of your strategy? Do they understand what the latest technology means in meeting the needs of your customers?

I offer the following three steps you can take today to inspire the heart and soul of your enterprise ...the people.

---

[1] *Source: Gallup Surveys February 2004 Chief Learning Officer magazine*

1. Employ the whole person
2. Leverage strengths for excellence
3. Plug into the power of alignment

Employ the whole person

People perform well when they feel well. One major impact on the way they feel at work is how their boss treats them. All too often, employees are seen as a means to an end rather than whole people. The number one reason employees leave organizations is their immediate supervisor. People don't leave companies—they leave managers!

Corporations spend much of their time and money making certain that high-level executives receive clear communication, knowledge of key strategies, and leadership grooming. This is good. Don't stop. My experience shows me that companies should also wake up to the fact that their front-line managers may have been promoted to the task without the requisite communication, team building and leadership training vital to their new roles.

Now that they must get the job done through others, being the top-skilled person in the department is no longer good enough. They must both manage things and lead people. Corporations that invest in the leadership skills of their managers will leverage their ability to inspire and engage all employees.

Organizations that realize these key people have the capacity to either inspire or deflate those they lead will become better at driving bottom-line results and meeting corporate objectives. These results will only be achieved through a commitment to training and development for managers.

It is critical that this investment in professional development be designed for meaningful results. It is my experience that workshops don't work. Many organizations offer a plethora of fragmented managerial and leadership skill classes. But, as Kirkpatrick and Kirkpatrick confirm, "There is a lot of great training material out there—information overload. [The training is] effective to *the degree that [it is] properly implemented.*"[2]

I have found success in pulling the material from such individual classes into a comprehensive program framed around the organization's

---

[2] Kirkpatrick & Kirkpatrick, Transforming Learning into Behavior, 2005

purpose, values and business goals. A program framed thusly and offered over an extended timeframe will have a lasting impact on the company culture and on the employees' learning. In other words, in order for learning to convert into the desired skills, attitudes and behaviors, adult learners must see the connection between the learning and the big picture. They must also have the opportunity to use classroom learning in real situations. I call this keeping the learning "on their mind while they are on the job."[3]

Nancy attended my management development program. She had been with her company for many years. This was her first opportunity to work on her professional development beyond the necessary certification courses for her trade. She arrived with a great attitude, but little knowledge of her company's vision. And, she did not have a practical strategy for using her unique personality style to lead others. She left with both.

At the end of the program she shared her realization—simple, yet oh so powerful: "Everyone has something different to offer, and what I have to offer is a valuable contribution. Now I feel like I can join in. I can play my part in the company's success." Our front-line managers need the investment in their development so that they can *join*. Only then will they be inspired and able to inspire those around them.

Here is another simple employee survey. Ask fifty people, "How are you?" Count the number of people that answer, "Busy!" I ask attendees in my keynote presentations to tell me how many of their fellow colleagues are tired, uninspired, or conspiring versus inspired. Tired is tied with uninspired for first place.

Another major impact on how we feel and, thus, perform is work-life balance. Some action must be taken to offset the busy times. Most employees would rather have time off the job than a raise!

Dave learned to treat the whole person and started his leadership tenure in the following manner. "I was a brand-new manager, and I had no experience other than I was brought up in the organization. For my first team meeting I booked the room for an hour and gave them a little background on myself, and then asked for a little of their background. Next I explained the team priorities: Family first. If you have a problem at home, you have to deal with that. If there's a basketball game or a ballet or something you

---

[3] Deborah J. Clifford, Manager to Leader Program: Learning Fundamentals, 2005

want to go to, leave and go to it. But, in turn, if there's a major project coming up, and we need you here on a Saturday, I expect you to be here." Setting these guidelines up front gained him respect and hard work from his team.

The data shows that overworked employees are simply not as productive as people who have better work-life balance. "The average American today is working 20 percent more hours than he or she did only fives years ago. That's a whole day a week. Fifty-seven percent are routinely at their desks from 50 to 65 hours a week."[4] "The cost of working marathon days is premature breakdown. Any engine that is constantly running will burn out."[5] Shortening the workday can boost performance. At the turn of the century, when factory workers put in long hours, shrinking the workday from 10 to 8 hours a day significantly increased productivity. Cutting the 40-hour workweek by up to 5 hours in the U.S. and Britain has led to less absenteeism, less turnover, less personal business on company time and lower costs.[6] Smart organizations will act on this data.

Some ideas that have paid off for organizations include: half-day Fridays in the summer (New York Life), giving employees more control over their own starting times and the ability to compress their workweeks (Xerox), splitting responsibility for evening work hours (Harris Bank), and four-day workweeks (Volkswagen A.G.). What creativity can you provide in this arena? Try something new, it will pay off.

Leverage strengths for excellence

The number one reason people look forward to working each day is to have the chance to realize their full potential.[7] Tapping into that potential means helping them find their strengths and then using those strengths to meet corporate objectives. Talent management today means playing the Matching Game with employee strengths and company needs.

Focusing on strengths can be compared to a jazz ensemble. The entire ensemble is working toward a single effect—great music. Each player

---

[4] *Fortune (November 30, 1992): p.64*

[5] Kriegel & Brandt, Sacred Cows Make the Best Burgers, 1996.

[6] *New York Times*, August 29, 1993), p. F9.

[7] *Sloan Management Review: Beyond The Paycheck*, Ian I. Mitroff & Elizabeth A. Denton,

knows his or her strengths (their instrument) and wouldn't think of using another instrument. Participants have a chance to shine—their solo. The trumpet player steps forward for a solo and steps back for the drummer's solo. The single effect desired in the organization is the achievement of the corporate goal. Leveraging strengths to get there takes the individual's wisdom and freedom to step forward for their solo and the grace to step back for another's time to employ their gifts and talents.

Yet our performance management systems often focus on employee weaknesses. The result is much time spent on improving something that is not natural to us and little time on fostering talents. Manage weaknesses just enough to avoid failure. Spend the rest of the time on pairing employee strengths to the tasks at hand. Managing weaknesses is achieved through both clever partnering and the more traditional route—skills training.

Help employees manage weaknesses through partnering with others who have strengths in their weak area(s). It takes courage and honest evaluation of one's strengths and weaknesses to ask a colleague for help. Once we do, we quickly learn that our colleagues may also need help in areas in which we are strong.

If managing employee weakness by partnering with others is not possible, then get them the requisite training and move on. Get those weaknesses out of the way and spend time nurturing people's strengths. The results will be amazing.

The next task is matching employee strengths with company needs. Philosopher Frederick Buechner said that your call in life is to find "the place where your deep gladness and the world's deep hunger meet." Exactly!

Early in my career I was a principal in a smaller company (120 employees). One of the advantages of a smaller and more nimble organization is the ability to maneuver the job roles and tasks to meet the talent and enthusiasm of the players. I remember spending hours in the president's office discussing individuals and their capabilities. We manipulated the roles, tasks and people like a giant Rubik's cube. The end result was a finely-honed corporate ensemble.

This Rubik's cube process can be formalized for larger companies. Matching employees' strengths to the company's needs supercharges the organization. The people are happy realizing their full potential and the company will have its passionate talents focused where they bring the most return.

Strengths-seekers can find assistance in a variety of ways from professional assessment tools to in-house or private coaching. Review the strengths matrix at the end of this chapter for one way to determine your likes and talents. Finding one's calling is no longer reserved for the unemployed or newly graduated. Organizations must assist employees in unearthing their gifts in order to bring them to work everyday.

Plug into the power of alignment

When employees' values are not aligned with corporate values, there is a huge disconnect. When the people in your company do not understand their role in achieving the ultimate purpose of your organization, they cannot produce an inspired result. How do your employees answer the question, "What do you do for a living"?

I remember fondly my first trip to St. Louis as president of my trade association. Our annual conference was held at the Adam's Mark Hotel in downtown St. Louis. Because I was in the volunteer position of board president, I was given the most extraordinary suite.

As I entered my room for the first time, a tour group joined me from a youth business club. Together we walked in awe past the chandeliers in the foyer to view two living rooms, a double-sided fireplace, baby grand piano, dining for twenty, and more.

One young lady on the tour couldn't help herself. She broke away from the group, came up to me, tapped my arm and asked in amazement, "Lady, what do you *DO* for a living?" I didn't have the heart to tell her I was "between jobs."

How corporate employees answer the question, "What do you do for a living?" provides insight into whether or not they are aligned with the company's purpose and values. Consider the following two dialogues:

What do you do for a living?
I am a leadership trainer for ABC Company.

vs.

What do you do for a living?
I help create leaders who inspire our organization. My company values their employees enough to provide continuous growth and development.

When employees' values and purpose are aligned with those of the organization, inspiration can occur. Without this alignment, tired, uninspired, and conspiring employees are more likely. Author Parker J. Palmer writes, "If the work we do lacks integrity for us, then we, the work, and the people we do it with will suffer."

In order to align and inspire others, make sure your organization's values and purpose are clearly articulated and authentically lived. Only then can people see if they are "a fit." Have you ever been in a job and just knew it was not a fit? You weren't sure why. The company may have been a good employer, but you felt you could not be yourself while at work. This is exactly what happens when employees do not feel aligned with the company's values and cause.

Take Wal-Mart for example. The company's purpose is to provide value and selection. All other things come second. If an employee values selling only the crème de la crème in product offerings, there will be a disconnect. How can employees with such a values mismatch put passion into their daily efforts? Clearly articulating the core ideology of the firm and allowing employees to understand how their values align with it builds commitment and inspiration.

Another example is Microsoft. The company's organizational culture revolves around getting leading-edge products out the door first. It is not unusual to spend long hours for weeks and months on projects. Exciting? To some. Not a great place to work if your primary value is work-life balance. Employees desiring such balance will quickly see they do not fit. However, there are many people who value the exhilaration and high activity levels, along with the financial rewards, of such an organizational culture.

Passionate and inspired employees are the result of a good match in values and purpose with those of their company. Careful attention must be paid to this in the hiring process. Be clear about your company culture, then hire and promote for it. Plug into the power of alignment.

R U Inspired?
R U Inspiring Others?

A leader must first be inspired. Only then can he or she inspire others. Are you inspired?

Ask yourself the following:

- What are your unique gifts & talents? ______________________

  ____

- Do you bring them to work? Yes No
- What are your values? Your organization's values? ______________________
____
- Are they aligned? Yes No
- What is your organization's cause? ______________________
____
- Are you drawn to it? Yes No
- Does it fit with your own purpose? Yes No

You owe it to yourself to be inspired. Your success as a leader depends on your ability to inspire others.

Remember these three steps to inspire others and boost profits:

1. Employ the whole person
2. Leverage strengths for excellence
3. Plug into the power of alignment

Finally, ask yourself at the end of each day "Who have I inspired today?" Because I learned ...it's the people, stupid!

Ten Tips For Finding & Using Your Strengths

1. Complete the strengths matrix below. View the list of strengths and accompanying matrix. Place each of your top ten strengths in the appropriate location on the matrix. Are you surprised?
2. Take a personality-type evaluator. We recommend Insights Discovery. This system produces a 23-page profile that includes a listing of your top ten strengths. Go to www.inspiredpeople.com to find out more.
3. Spend 15-30 minutes journaling at the end of each day. Purchase a notebook or journal. Review your day. Write down the areas where your talents showed up.
4. Hire a personal coach. Coaches help you meet your goals. They will also help clarify your talents and gifts by encouraging reflection and offering feedback.
5. Reflect on your past. Document the high points by creating a timeline. Highlight milestones where you where "in the zone." What where you doing at these times? You may see a trend that shows your strengths.
6. Attend a retreat. Sometimes all it takes is a commitment to uninterrupted time to reflect. Check out local retreats or workshops that encourage quiet activities. Make a date with yourself to attend.
7. Solicit feedback from colleagues. Colleagues can be a great source of information. Ask them what they perceive your strengths to be.
8. Throw a party. Invite friends and family over. Ask them to each bring a "gift." The gift is an index card with one or two talents they see in you.
9. Revisit your performance reviews. Your last several performance reviews are worth another look. Take note of your strengths. Jot them down on a separate list and hang them in a highly visible location.
10. Ask your mother. What would/does your mother say? When all else fails, mother knows best. The older I get, the more I know she is right, don't you?

STRENGTHS MATRIX

Circle your top ten strengths from the list below. You may add a different strength if you do not see it listed. Next, plot your strengths on the matrix on the following page. Place them according to your overall use of the strength on the job as well as the 'fit' needed for your current duties. If many of your top ten strengths are both highly used and a good fit for your job, you are bringing your strengths to work each day.

Use = I use this strength.

Fit = My strength is a fit for my job duties/role.

Original thinker

Highly resourceful

Good listener

Great with details

Forward-looking thinker

Can help others achieve their goals

A sound sense of duty

Help create a sense of unity on the team

Sensible

Realistic

Systematic

Quick thinker

Happy to serve others

Sensitive to the needs of others

Articulate communicator

Effective in relationships

Constant source of fun

Self-disciplined

Keen observer

Natural go-getter

Pragmatic

Find better ways to get things done

Help folks work more efficiently

Boundless energy

Juggle many roles simultaneously

Diplomatic

Change agent

Good situational analysis

Analytical

Great networker

Conceptual thinker (see the big picture)

Competitive

Loyal to fellow team members

Brave & daring

Encouraging to others

Solid organizational abilities

Quietly productive

Adaptable

Self-reliant

Do not accept 2nd best

Disciplined

Bring order and structure to projects

Great planning abilities

Innovative

Collaborative

Creative thinker

Strong task focus

Accountable

Trustworthy

Consistent performer

Hi

Low use – Good fit	***High use – Good fit***
Low use – Poor fit	***High use – Poor fit***

Lo

CHAPTER EIGHT

Winning Business

Driving results by engaging employees

Bill Fotsch

Bill Fotsch is the Head Coach for The Great Game of Business, Inc. In 1994, Bill started the coaching business to help companies improve their financial results and the lives of the employees who drive those results. Since then, he has worked with over 100 different companies in a wide variety of industries. The companies range from small, privately held companies, to mid-sized companies, to Fortune 500 firms, including Southwest Airlines, Harley Davidson, Roadway Express and Capital One.

Prior to starting in the coaching business, Bill had over 20 years of business experience as a results-oriented manager with a successful track record of improving company sales and profits in a broad array of industries. A much sought after speaker, Bill has spoken in a wide variety of settings, from annual meetings and national conferences to CEO groups. He has been a guest lecturer at the University of Chicago Business School. He serves on the board of directors of several companies, all of which practice the Great Game of Business.

Bill received his bachelor's degree in Mechanical Engineering from Marquette University and his master's degree in Business Administration from Harvard Business School, where he graduated as a Baker Scholar. Bill and his wife, Joy, and three children live in the Cincinnati suburb of Villa Hills, Kentucky. Bill's commitment to faith, family and friends provide a strong motivation for his work, tempered with a sense of humor that helps him avoid taking himself too seriously.

The Great Game of Business
Springfield, MO • (417) 831-7706 • bfotsch@ggob.com

Bill Fotsch

Winning Business

Driving results by engaging employees

How would you like to compete with a company whose employees are *fully* engaged in the business? All of the employees understand how the business works and what is critical for success. They regularly track results and continually think about how they could improve those results. Because they have a common goal and incentives tied to that goal, they easily collaborate between departments, focusing their energies on serving their customers substantially better than the competition. And because they openly discuss wins and losses, they keep learning and getting better.

Sound like a tough competitor? I'll bet it does. Does it sound like your organization? If so, you have my compliments. If time permits, please get in touch with me. I would like to learn more about what you are doing. If this doesn't sound like your company, this chapter will give you some ideas about moving in that direction.

Background

From 1975 through 1994, in a variety of operating roles in four different companies, I saw first-hand the power of teams and engaged employees. I also saw how much is lost when employees are not engaged. From 1994 to the present, I have worked with more than 100 different companies to improve their business results and the lives of their employees by engaging them in the business; through the management process Jack Stack calls "The Great Game of Business." Stack is the president of SRC, a very successful employee-owned company that is a former division of International

Harvester. SRC, like many of the companies I have worked with (including Southwest Airlines, Kinko's, Harley-Davidson, Roadway Express, Green Mountain Coffee Roasters, and Universal Engineering), generates great business results by getting its employees engaged and "into the game."

Two world-class examples of companies that engage their employees are Southwest Airlines and Harley-Davidson. I have had the privilege of working with both companies. Over the years, both of these companies' stocks have outperformed that of their respective competitors'. Both companies have left the competition far behind. Their successful business performance is driven by many factors, but one thing they have in common is a pervasive culture of ownership among their employees. Having employees who are more engaged in the business gives them competitive advantages that bolster their business results.

I have asked many managers, owners, and front-line employees the following simple question: Who is better off when a company's employees are really engaged in the business—the customers, the owners, the managers, or the employees? I know they get it when they respond "everyone." This is an important step. You want to be sure that your employees understand that having them fully engaged in the business is in everyone's best interest—except the competition's.

At some level, you would think this is obvious, right? Unfortunately, to many employees it is not obvious. Employees may be immersed in the conventional wisdom that business is evil and profits are bad. Reading the paper or listening to television, they are bombarded with stories about corruption in business—stories like Enron, WorldCom, etc. It's a dog-eat-dog world out there, and in business you either focus on profits at the expense of the people, or people at the expense of profits. It takes time for them to consider that there might be a better way, one in which both the business and the employees benefit. Countering the bad publicity with examples of industry-leading companies operating in a way that benefits both business and workers, helps employees discover the wisdom of getting engaged in the business.

But then you have to deal with the next question: *How* do I get everyone engaged in the business? Many companies have tried to get their employees more engaged through some sort of profit-sharing plan or by giving them stock or options in the company. While well-intentioned, these moves are rarely effective, since the employees often have little understanding of how they might affect the company's profits or how they can influence the value of the stock.

How to Get Started: Define Winning

We spend *a lot* of time telling people that business is a game. It has players, rules, winners and losers, and rewards depending on performance. Played well, it's a great game. Each company has its own set of challenges, regulations, competitors, customer requirements, technology, and so on. And the key business challenges change over time. A good starting point is to figure out what *winning* means in your business right now, based on the most important issues you face.

In 1983, when SRC was starting out, the company had a huge problem. In a desperate effort to save jobs, the 13 senior managers purchased the business from International Harvester for $9 million. Since they did not have a great deal of personal wealth, they had to borrow most of the money. They financed the purchase with $8.9 million dollars of debt at the *deal* interest rate of 22 percent. Even so, the bank fired the loan officer for making such a high-risk loan. But the company's biggest weakness became the company's biggest strength. Those same managers got their employees focused on making the bank loan payment each month, and that became their unifying goal. Internal bickering substantially diminished as employees worked toward making that monthly payment. Through hard work and an engaged workforce focused on a common goal, a very unlikely success story emerged.

Since 1994 I have worked in partnership with SRC to apply these principles at other companies. You can start the process of engaging employees in the business by seeking their input on key issues the company faces. Asking for their input through an anonymous survey is a great start, because it begins to engage them. If the survey questions are relevant and important, it also is a powerful tool for influencing employee behavior. (For more on the power of thoughtful questions, I suggest you look into the topic of Appreciative Inquiry.)

In similar fashion, it is important to get the input of the management team. See what they understand to be the biggest opportunities and challenges, and if the managers and the employees have similar perspectives. We combine the input of employees and managers with a financial trend analysis and input from the marketplace—particularly customers and competitors. By looking at a company from these four perspectives, you can quickly get a sound understanding of the issues facing the business, and the likelihood that you will miss some key problem or opportunity is small.

After completing this initial homework, which we call the appraisal process, summarize the key issues that emerge. For example, you may have a shortage of sales and excess capacity. Perhaps costs are too high in relation to a competitor that uses new technology. Maybe your employees are unhappy and turnover is driving up costs for hiring and training. Below is a summary of the key issues of one company we worked with, a manufacturer of specialty gears:

Employees:
- ***Morale was low; wages had been cut 10%***
- ***Employees were still committed to the company***
- ***Little to no understanding of the business financials***

Customers:
- ***Pleased with company's quality and price***
- ***Not satisfied with on- time delivery performance***

Financials:
- ***Losses were mounting; scrap was high***
- ***Excessive overtime created high costs***
- ***High inventory hurt cash flow and required debt***

From the key issues identified, develop one or two metrics that define winning for the next six to twelve months. (See the Worksheet at the end of this chapter.) That is your critical number: an objective measure that defines winning in the short term. For SRC in 1983, the critical number was making the bank loan payment. Depending on the nature of your business and the issues you face, it may be revenue per employee, room occupancy, or cost per unit. For the specialty gear manufacturer I mentioned earlier, the critical number became manpower efficiency. Manpower efficiency was defined as:

$$\frac{\textit{Gears Shipped x Standard Hours}}{\textit{Total Paid Hours}}$$

Look back at the issues faced by this gear manufacturer. See how improvements in manpower efficiency would tend to have a positive influence on each of those issues. Fortunately, manpower efficiency was something with which employees were already familiar. As your employees become more financially literate, the critical number may become gross margin or return on assets. This becomes the central focus of the company over the next six to twelve months, much as making the bank loan payment was in the early days of SRC. Creating a clear, common definition of winning for all employees will have a powerful effect on teamwork and communications for your business.

(Note for larger companies: If you have more than 1000 employees, it helps to break your company structure down into smaller business units or natural teams. After that, the process for larger companies and smaller companies is pretty much the same.)

Making Results Visible: Scoreboard

If employees have helped you define winning measures, they are already more engaged in the business. To take things to the next level, make that company-wide definition of winning visible on an ongoing basis and let them see how they can affect the results. Put up a scoreboard so everybody sees how the company is doing. The summary of key issues you identified helps define the biggest drivers of the critical number, and the aim is to make those drivers visible. Create a clear "line of sight" for all employees, so they can see company performance and how they influence the overall results. A good scoreboard reflects the company's organizational chart rather than a financial statement, enabling each department or group within the company to see the impact of its actions. Graphing overall results, showing actual performance versus a baseline (such as the budget or last year's results) can clarify this line of sight.

Operating Profit

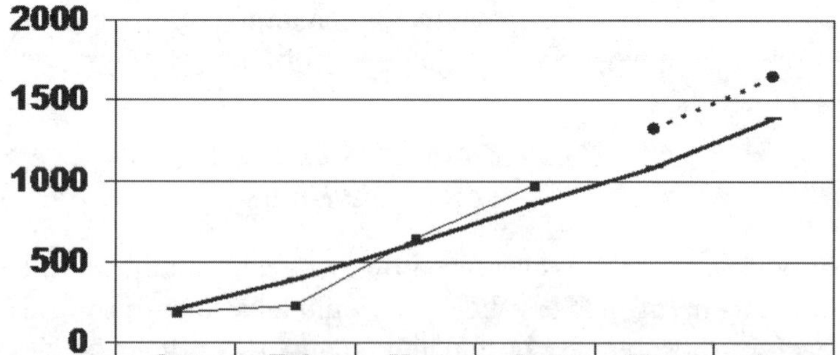

	Jan	Feb	Mar	Apr	May	Jun
Budget	209	393	610	856	1,089	1,385
Actual	186	227	643	975		
Forecast					1,323	1,649

This graph is a good example of a graphic scoreboard from an engineering services company where the critical number was operating profit. Everyone can see that the company got off to a slow start, as actual results were below budget for the first two months. But March and April were very strong months and, as a result, the company is now performing above plan. Simple, right? At a glance, everyone can see that the company came from behind and is now winning versus budget.

You will then want to create a regular forum during which results can be reviewed, progress celebrated, variances identified, and everyone kept current. It works well to have a short meeting, 30 minutes or so, once a week, to review results. This is not a problem-solving meeting. The purpose is to track company performance, learn from what happened the past week, and identify needed adjustments. Get employees thinking ahead about what they can do to affect results. Have them forecast expected monthly results in their area of responsibility. Record the forecast on the graphical scoreboard. Here is how a landscape company implemented its forecast of gross margin dollars, their critical number.

Owner	*Bill*	*Mary*	*George*	*John*	*Frank*	
Revenue:	**Landscape**	**Nursery**	**Com. Maint.**	**Residential**	**Tree Shrub**	**Total**
Budget	$154,500	$37,000	$225,000	$52,000	$4,000	$568,082
Forecast	***$147,250***	***$34,000***	***$280,000***	***$50,000***	***$11,300***	***$607,550***
Expenses:	**Landscape**	**Nursery**	**Com. Maint.**	**Residential**	**Tree Shrub**	**Total**
Labor Budget	24,200	6,600	73,713	16,500	594	136,326
Labor Forecast	***22,500***	***6,800***	***85,000***	***15,500***	***1,356***	***141,356***
Materials Budget	36,000	800	1,500	1,407	2,775	49,137
Materials Forecast	***33,000***	***1,500***	***3,500***	***1,525***	***1,530***	***49,160***
Gross Margin:	**Landscape**	**Nursery**	**Com. Maint.**	**Residential**	**Tree Shrub**	**Total**
Budget	$94,300	$29,600	$149,787	$34,093	$631	$382,619
Forecast	***$91,750***	***$25,700***	***$191,500***	***$32,975***	***$8,414***	***$417,034***
Actual						

Notice how the overall company performance is divided into various teams. Each team can see how they are affecting overall company performance. Identifying component performance provides a higher level of *ownership* of results. Why forecast? Because it encourages employees to think about cause and effect—that is, how they can influence the numbers rather than just passively looking at results to date. It takes discipline to learn this skill, but it is powerful.

Each week get an update from the employees on monthly expected results. The meeting goes quickly, since their forecast may often be simply "no change." However, when forecasts do change, there is something to be learned. Encourage employees to provide a brief explanation of why they changed their forecast, so everyone may absorb the lesson. When actual results are available at the end of the month, compare forecasts to actual results and discuss variances. This process facilitates additional learning and gives you a clear idea of who is on top of their part of the business and who needs help.

(Note: Convinced that forecasting is impossible in your business? If so, get in touch and I will forward the contact information for some company presidents who were once just as convinced and are now reaping the benefits of weekly forecasts.)

Aligning Employee Incentives: Bonus Plan

Once you have defined winning and implemented results tracking, and employees see how they can affect those results, provide an incentive tied to the same "critical number." The incentive should be self-funded from the incremental dollars generated by improvements in business results. For smaller companies, I recommend employees participate in a company-wide incentive plan, reinforcing the importance of the team. For larger companies, the team may be a business unit or a particular geographic office. Reinforce the linkage between company winning and the employees winning. Rest assured that the scoreboard will make it very apparent who is driving results and who is not. And because everyone shares in the company's wins, all members of the team are encouraged to contribute.

A great way to make the bonus visible and demonstrate that it is being funded by the teams' efforts is to tie the updated forecasts on the critical number to their effect on the anticipated bonus. As forecasts on the critical number move up or down, so does the forecasted bonus. This reinforces teamwork. Operations forecasts an increase in efficiency, improving the critical number forecast, and everyone's bonus is increased. The sales team is able to increase the price on a key product, increasing the critical number, and everyone's bonus is increased. Lose a customer and everyone's bonus is reduced.

Some may think that the rewards should go directly to the individuals who are generating significant improvements. In the long run, this tends to be the case with promotions and increases in compensation. I believe the majority of bonus plans should be team- based to reinforce good team behavior. After all, business is a team sport. Any salesperson going after a new account with many great references knows that most of his or her success is due to operations creating delighted customers.

Implementation: Setting a Timetable

Below is a typical implementation timetable.

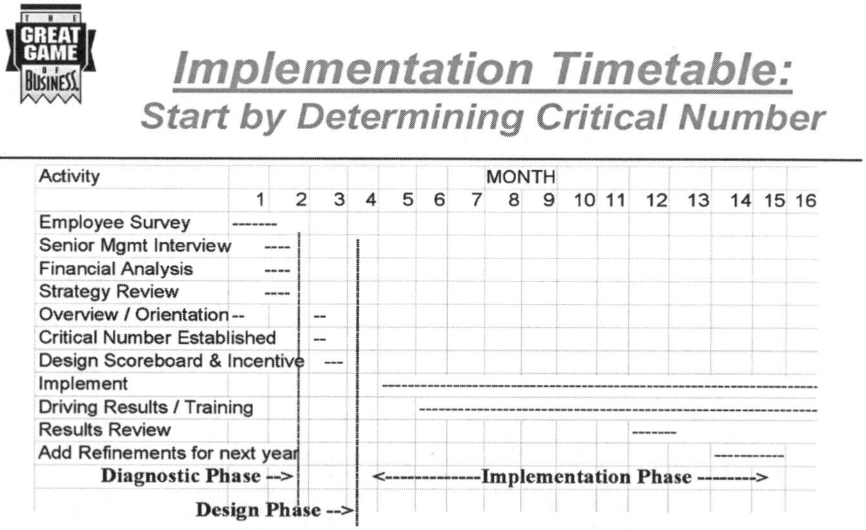

Copyright Great Game of Business

Note that in this chapter I focused on the initial diagnostic and design portions of engaging employees. Ongoing implementation and driving of results should flow from the weekly meetings. As opportunities or variances present themselves, there are natural learning opportunities. Take advantage of these opportunities to recognize accomplishments. Recognition frequently means more to the employees than whatever incremental level of compensation came from the results. Going forward, engage employees in making refinements to the critical number, scoreboards and incentive plans for the next year, as part of the planning and budgeting process.

Are you ready to start winning the game?

Are you going to get started so you can reap the rewards of having more engaged employees? I hope you do. Don't be afraid of making mistakes. You will—and so will your employees. But you will learn from those mistakes and make progress along the way. The only real mistake is not moving forward. You can lead your industry in reaping the benefits of engaged employees or you can follow. You can be the Southwest Airlines of your industry or the TWA. Being Southwest is more fun. Good luck.

Winning Business Worksheet

What are the most important (key) issues you face?

____

____

____

____

____

____

____

____

From the key issues identified, develop one or two metrics that define winning for the next six to twelve months.

____

____

____

____

____

____

____

____

CHAPTER NINE

What the Heck Happened?

When bad behavior happens to good people

Susan Meyer-Miller

As an international speaker, Susan Miller has trained and motivated a half-million people in eight countries. She is a published author, a small business owner and an occasional business commentator on Fox News.

After earning a B.A. in Human Resources Management, Susan began her career in the restaurant business building and leading teams. Her motto is *"let's get the job done and still have fun!"* As Training Manager for the world's largest Pizza Hut franchise, she guided all levels of training for 450 restaurants, managed the corporate training center, and published the company newsletter. In 1990, Susan joined Fred Pryor Seminars as a speaker and began an eight-year adventure of travel, teaching, and discovery.

In 1995, upon finding herself suffering from "frequent flier fallout," she regained life balance by taking her career into her own hands and starting SpeakerUSA. She has become "The Customizer," creating motivational training programs specifically geared to help clients meet their business challenges head-on.

Today SpeakerUSA, Inc. boasts over 100 clients, including HR Block, Life Fitness, and the Missouri Realtors Association. Susan brings fun and laughter into her programs and is a favorite speaker at conventions and conferences nationwide.

SpeakerUSA, Inc.
Shawnee, KS • 877-674-8446 • www.speakerusa.com

Susan Meyer-Miller

What the Heck Happened?

When bad behavior happens to good people

Have you ever looked back on a meeting or workplace conversation and asked yourself, "What the heck happened there?" Are you perplexed by the not-so-pleasing personalities at work who put a hex on your productivity? Does your blood boil when you have to deal with the difficult, dysfunctional and demented?

Well, you're not alone. Many highly effective professionals find themselves in a conundrum when challenged by the antisocial behaviors and crazy communication strategies of difficult people. Communication skills that work just fine with most people are often ineffective with **D**ifficult, **R**ude, and **I**rritating **P**eople. But never fear: there *are* proven tactics that *really work* if you are willing to deal with DRIPs and use the tactics consistently.

This chapter will give you confidence in handling challenging people by first helping you discover your own "hot buttons" and vulnerabilities in dealing with DRIP behavior. You will gain valuable insight into what makes DRIPs tick and how to respond to their bad behavior with proven tactics that minimize negative workplace impact.

Difficult or Just Different?

DRIPs are frustrating people who chronically stand in the way of you doing your job effectively. Let's use the 3 Cs to define a DRIP. DRIPs:

- Cause problems,
- Consistently cause problems, and there is a
- Consensus about the fact they cause problems!

If someone you know fits this description, then read on. It's not just a personality clash. You can create a powerful strategy to handle DRIPs and get the results you deserve.

Preparing Yourself to Address Bad Behavior

Relationships with DRIPs are often unproductive and confusing. DRIPs operate from a different "rule book" and often exhibit challenging behaviors or unfriendly tactics when interacting with others. They behave this way because it works—they have been rewarded over and over for behaving badly (they get their way, shirk responsibility, etc.). If you are unprepared to address the bad behavior, you will find yourself being manipulated, controlled or outmaneuvered. Remember: doing nothing sends a message that the bad behavior is acceptable.

Breaking an unhealthy pattern with a DRIP requires insight, energy, and assertiveness. Some of the recommended counter-tactics may be outside your comfort zone, and you may think some of them even border on rude. But these tactics work, so prepare to meet the challenge head on. Let's start with a self-analysis and a few basic principles so you work from strength when dealing with DRIPs.

Assess your conflict style

You have developed your approach to conflict over a lifetime. You watch parents and people you admire interact with others. You are rewarded or punished for certain behaviors at home, school, and in other social groups. You develop your own approach to working through conflict with others and often repeat patterns whether they work or not.

To deal with challenging people you must first become aware of your habitual response patterns during conflict. What is working? What isn't? What do you do with the pent up energy when you are angry or frustrated? Look at the three styles in the following table. Which style best describes your typical approach to conflict?

Stuffing	Directing	Escalating
• Passive: gives in to keep the peace	• Assertive: seeks a win-win	• Aggressive: attacks under stress
• Avoids conflict	• Confronts unfair practices	• Displays negative emotions
• "Bottles" the negative energy	• Uses excess energy to work toward a solution	• Yells, may use profanity or name calling
• Defers decisions to others	• Stands up for ideas	• Interrupts
• Builds resentment when things don't go their way	• Maintains self-control	• Exaggerates
• Talks about issues to everyone but the source of the problem	• Takes ownership for outcomes	• Places blame
• "Poor me" mentality	• Tells the truth	• "I'm OK—You're not" attitude

Difficult people often push our buttons and send us to extremes. We wind up "stuffing" anger away or "escalating" the discussion, resulting in a less than ideal outcome. Although it is natural during a conflict to go into a "fight or flight" response, this is often the wrong way to counteract bad behavior. You will get the best results with DRIPs by "directing" your emotions appropriately, maintaining self-control and choosing your responses carefully, letting them know you can't be pushed or manipulated and that you expect them to act fairly and with respect.

Determine your "soft spots"

What are your personal vulnerabilities that work against you when dealing with DRIPs? Do any of these reactions sound like you?

- *Guilt* – You fall for the heavy sigh or lines like "If you really cared about…"
- *Competitiveness* – You can't stand to be second best. When you find yourself the victim of bad behavior you create a win-lose situation, which may exacerbate the situation or bring out the really nasty side of the DRIP.
- *Fear of confrontation* – You are uncomfortable with standing your ground or asking the DRIP to treat you differently. You would rather give in or avoid them.
- *Short Fuse* – You let the DRIP get to you, causing you to lose control. Both parties are now embroiled in a childish fight or workplace rivalry and nothing is resolved. Another possible consequence of a short fuse is the DRIP turns the situation against you by shining a spotlight on your aggressive behavior, taking the focus off of the problem that caused the outburst in the first place.
- *Thin Skinned* – You are easily offended and focused on how *you* are being treated. You get defensive and want the DRIP to change (which is not going to happen).
- *Perfectionism* – If you want it done right, do it yourself. Watch out—DRIPS will let *you* do the work. Often a perfectionist in need of superior results will work around a DRIP rather than taking the time and energy to confront them about doing their fair share.

Be conscious of your "hot buttons"

…and don't let DRIPs push them! What are the specific things these challenging people do or say that set you off? Make a list of these emotional "triggers" and work to avoid knee-jerk reactions that make the situation worse when DRIPs exhibit bad behavior.

Are any of these your "hot buttons"?

People who never take responsibility for their mistakes
A whiny or condescending tone of voice
Someone who says "What-*everrr*"
Eye-rolling in a meeting
Subtle or not-so-subtle put-downs

Remember that DRIPs usually communicate from a point of weakness. Insecurities hide behind their bad behavior. Once you realize this, it is easy to handle them with a sort of detachment. Accept who they are and don't let the behavior get under your skin.

Determine the DRIP's "payoff"

Why do DRIPs continue behaving badly? You would think they'd get a clue the behavior is unwelcome because of the conflict they experience (and how often they change jobs!). Unfortunately, DRIPs are behaviorally blind. They have no idea the impact they have on others. As long as they get their payoff, they will continue the rude behavior.

Think about children who throw tantrums. If you give in and give them what they want, they will continue to act out. If you ignore the behavior or break the pattern with an unwanted outcome, they will realize the bad behavior has no effect and eventually become well-adjusted adults who know how to get what they need without behaving badly. The secret is to identify DRIPs' motivators and then withhold the payoff to teach them how to treat you.

Power Principles for Coping With DRIPs

To work from strength with a DRIP, you must have an analytical view of people. Here are a few truths to keep in mind when you are dealing with bad behavior.

"*Situations are transitional.*" Just because the DRIP starts a conversation displaying rude behavior doesn't mean he or she will continue to be rude. The way *you respond* to the challenging behavior determines your outcome. There are *many* ways to respond to a person. Stop and think about your options before responding to a DRIP.

"*No one can make you feel inadequate without your consent.*" These famous words spoken by Eleanor Roosevelt are truly empowering.

No one can *make* you mad or sad or glad. Only you can decide how a DRIP will affect you. We all assign meaning to events that happen to us—sometimes positivcly, sometimes negatively. The way you define an event with a DRIP might be distorted, creating an emotional "trigger" that leads to an unproductive response. For instance, when someone uses a condescending tone, you might feel put down or insulted, when in fact they may be more focused on how smart they look and are trying to convince you and everyone else (including themselves) they're OK. Be careful not to distort the meaning of events when dealing with bad behavior.

"It always gets worse before it gets better." When you begin standing up to DRIPs, refusing to give them the payoff, they will often ramp up the challenging behavior in desperation. Once they realize you won't put up with bad behavior and expect to be treated with respect, they will give up the negative behavior. It may take five to seven interactions before the DRIP gets the point.

"Intermittent reinforcement is the most powerful." This means that once you have reestablished the ground rules of your relationship with the DRIP, if you slack off once and give them the "payoff," you will probably find yourself back to square one. It is best to teach DRIPs how to treat you by using the tactics in this chapter consistently.

"You won't change the DRIP, but you can teach him how to treat you." This means there is no magic technique that will make a selfish, egotistical jerk into a nice person. What you *can* do is use these techniques to minimize the difficult behavior when the person is interacting with you.

Real World Tactics for Dealing With DRIPs

There are many different types of difficult people, but in this chapter we only address the most common. Sometimes the DRIP is a combination of several types, so it is helpful to know and use a specific formula when dealing with *any* kind of DRIP. You can use this formula to handle the difficult people who are not discussed in the book. We will start with this five-step formula and then meet a few of the most common DRIPs and learn strategies to banish their bad behavior.

Step 1. **Pinpoint the challenging behavior.** List the things the DRIP does or says that trigger an emotional response from you.

Step 2. **Uncover the "payoff"** the DRIP receives when exhibiting this behavior.

Step 3. **Determine your objective.** What are you trying to accomplish in the interactions? Are you trying to get them to listen to your ideas? Stop interrupting? Stop sabotaging your leadership? Quit shooting down ideas in meetings?

Step 4. **Choose your attitude.** You always have several ways of looking at a situation. For instance, if you heard someone was saying negative things about you, you might confront them with anger (aggressive) or hurt feelings (passive), or you might approach them with the attitude that you are open to any feedback they have to give and that you want to make sure they realize you value their working relationship.

Step 5. **Plan and implement your strategy.** Determine the best approach to dealing with the person. Mentally rehearse the interactions including specific phrases and possible scenarios before confronting the person. Afterward, evaluate how well it worked and adjust your approach for the next interaction. Keep trying new things until something works.

Meet Some Common DRIPs

"The Intimidator"

Bad Behavior: Intimidators are aggressive. When presenting ideas they state opinions as fact. They are poor listeners and often judgmental of any idea not their own. Intimidators will argue, humiliate, interrupt and talk over others to be in control. If publicly embarrassed, Intimidators can become vindictive. Although Intimidators see themselves as nice, they can be short-tempered and quick to attack, keeping others on unsure ground.

Payoff: Getting their way. Gaining control.

Your Objective(s): Stand your ground; get them to listen.

Strategy: When interacting with this person, stay detached and never take anything they do or say personally. Don't let your voice tone sound like they are getting to you. Don't put yourself down or give in too easily. Never get into an argument or humiliate the Intimidator. Watch *their* ego but never let *yours* get in the way—especially if you're the boss.

Stand your ground in discussions with the Intimidator. Mirror their body language, using the space with the same bravado. Deepen your voice tone and don't let them interrupt. When an Intimidator butts in during a meeting, avoid looking their way and use a soft "stop" or "just a minute" motion with your hand.

"Excuse me, I wasn't quite finished. As I was saying…"

"Bob I want to hear your ideas, but first let me finish my thought." (*Don't* end with "Okay?")

Instead of arguing with an Intimidator, use questions to guide them to your point of view:

"Sounds like you put a lot of thought into it. What is your plan for handling (the problem)…?"

"How do you think that will affect the accounting department?"

"Have you talked to Leticia about this? What do you think her opinion would be?"

When there is a stalemate or the conversation becomes heated, call a timeout.

"Well, it looks like we have a stalemate here. Why don't we both think about it and figure out a way to compromise. Let's meet…"

"Back Stabber"

Bad Behavior: Backstabbers like to put others down *indirectly*—when you are not around to counter their comments—or by cloaking the dig in humor hoping you will laugh along. They instigate trouble within the group and hook people with a bit of truth along with the ugly stuff. When Back Stabbers are confronted, they deny any wrongdoing: " *It must have been a misunderstanding," or "I never said that."*

Payoffs: Building themselves up by putting others down. Secrecy. Sabotage.

Your Objective(s): To get them to stop stabbing you in the back and deal with problems authentically.

Strategy: Confront the Back Stabber directly *every time* you hear they have said something negative about you. Remember, they like to hide out and are uncomfortable with direct confrontation. Normally it is best to speak to them in private, but if the bad behavior happens in a group and is masked by humor, enlist the group as they have.

"Maria, I heard you were upset by my decision to..."

"Maurice, I heard through the grapevine you didn't like..."

"I am detecting some resentment. Is there something I need to know?"

"Chris, you're so funny! Seriously, though, do any of you really feel that way?"

Expect Backstabbers to deny any bad behavior when confronted. Allow the denial, indicating that if they *do* have issues, you are willing to discuss them openly. If they ask your source, don't it give up.

"It doesn't really matter who told me; what is more important to me is that you feel comfortable coming to me with any issues. I value our working relationship."

"That's good. I'm glad you didn't say it, and I want you to know you can come to me if you have problems, and I will do the same for you."

The Back Stabber *will* strike again. Continue to confront the bad behavior *every* time it surfaces. Act as if the second, fourth or seventh time you confront them is the very first time without mentioning prior discussions. Keep your voice tone positive and matter of fact. Once Back Stabbers realize they can't hide, the group is not playing along, and they can't sabotage your reputation, the bad behavior will stop.

Note to Managers: When a Back Stabber comes to you about a co-worker, your role is to bring about professional, truthful communication. Coach the person to deal directly with problems or mediate between the two people. Don't go to the other person individually because they will have a completely different perspective. The truth is somewhere in between, and the best way to get to it is to get the people together. The conversation might go like this:

"When you talked to Jean about that what did she say?"
(I didn't.)

"If Jean came to me with an issue about you without giving you a chance to handle it first, how would you feel?"
(I guess I wouldn't like it very much.)

"Why don't you have a chat with Jean and see if you can work it out. Can I give you a few pointers about how to say it?"
(I could *never* do that. or She wouldn't listen.)

"Let's get Jean in here to discuss it."
(No! Don't go get her!)

"When you bring me these issues, I feel like I need to address them. If you are not willing to deal with Jean directly does that mean it isn't such a big problem?"

"The Cynical Complainer"

Bad Behavior: The Complainer finds fault with everything and everyone around them and they must tell others about it. They often take on a whiny or angry tone—they go on and on and on. They tend to be blamers and will shoot down new ideas with all kinds of reasons why they won't work. Sometimes the Complainer is a great worker or a long-term employee whom others listen to.

Payoff: When others listen or agree.

Your Objective(s): To get them to be part of the solution or stop wasting your time.

Strategy: Don't spend a lot of time with the Complainer or try to offer solutions. They are not looking for ways to fix problems; they just want to complain. Ask a Cynical Complainer for solutions or ask them to come up with new ideas instead of the ones they shot down. When a Complainer sits down in front of you to vent, don't just listen and nod—hoping they will go away. It is better to state a time limit or use cut-offs if they corner you.

"That's a tough situation. What are you going to do about it?"

"I only have a couple of minutes. What specifically can I do to help you?"

"I don't agree. I think..."

"What do you recommend?"

"What have you tried that does work?"

Once the Complainer realizes you are not going to give them time for negativity, they will stop wasting yours. When they realize that you are going to expect them to be part of the solution, the bad behavior will subside.

"The Critical Know-It-All"

Bad Behavior: Critics come off as conceited know-it-alls. They are condescending, closed-minded and stubborn. They often torpedo discussions with loads of data to make their points. Critics point out what's wrong and always have to be right. They have a hard time listening to others and do not take coaching well. Most Critics—although they seem full of themselves—are really insecure. They are trying to convince themselves and everyone else they are OK.

Payoff: Making themselves look (and feel) smarter. Getting you to feel stupid.

Your Objective(s): To convey a confident and prepared image.

Strategy: When dealing with Critics, recognize them for their expertise while at the same time showing you have done your homework. Avoid taking the Critic's comments personally or appearing defensive. Acknowledge the Critic but don't feel obligated to agree or to commit to changing your way of doing things. It is not necessary to agree or disagree with them—just let them know you heard them. Prepare yourself for discussions with facts and references rather than opinions. Put your counterpoints in the form of questions, as you would with an Intimidator.

"So you think it would be a good idea to...I hear you. Anything else?"

"It is possible we need to look into that. Thanks for the input."

I was told to do it this way. Is that in the policy manual?"

"Steve, since you are the one most interested in the______ , why don't you take that on as your project."

Some Final Thoughts

DRIPs can be a drag. But you *can* minimize their impact with a straightforward approach and an assertive attitude. Don't let DRIPs get to you. Rise above the bad behavior and confront it head on. It may take a while, but when the DRIP isn't getting the payoff, they no longer want to play the game...at least not with you!

CHAPTER TEN

Inspiring Others to Reach the Summit

Using Appreciative Inquiry and coaching skills to build partnerships with employees

David E. Nelson, D.MIN.

Dr. David Nelson has been leading himself and others for all of his adult life. He is part of the movement for human liberation. In his relationship with a great diversity of people he recognizes a mysterious and wonderful human connection. Through The Human Agenda, Dr. Nelson continues his lifelong passion to live fully and invite others to live fully. He provides resources and coaching for people and organizations to claim their full human potential. He is a personal empowerment coach, motivational speaker, consultant, and trainer.

Recent clients include Head Start programs throughout the United States, United States Department of Health and Human Services, Emergency Medicine Leadership programs through Fitch and Associates, and a variety of school districts and collaborations. He partners with leadership teams as well as individuals to discover, celebrate and nurture what is best in them.

David's programs on TEAMS, *Appreciative Supervision*, and *Appreciative Parenting* have been enthusiastically received in over 35 states. As a distributor for Inscape he provides training on DiSC and other profile learning instruments.

The most requested topics include team building, emotional intelligence, appreciative inquiry, supervision, and leadership. His passion for people, energy for getting the task completed, and human leadership skills enable him to support you in being the wonderful human beings you really are.

The Human Agenda
Kansas City, MO • (816) 453-3835 • www.humanagenda.com

David E. Nelson, D.MIN.

Inspiring Others to Reach the Summit

Using Appreciative Inquiry and coaching skills to build partnerships with employees

Bear Butte is a sacred mountain among the Sioux, Cheyenne, and other Indian peoples. It is located just north of Sturgis, South Dakota. Legends abound about this mountain on the prairie. Some say that Crazy Horse was born at the base of the mountain. Many say he did his vision quests on the mountain. Some even say that his body is buried here. Legends aside, the place is sacred. Native people make pilgrimages there to pray and listen. Today it is a state park and the public is invited to walk the trail to the summit, but cautioned not to touch or tamper with any of the sacred objects hanging from the trees. Several years ago a forest fire stripped the trees of their green and the look is even more mystical than before.

Recently, I had the opportunity to walk the trail with some Alaskan Natives and American Indian friends. We got to Bear Butte about 6:15 in the evening and we needed to allow two hours to get to the top. I wanted to get as far as possible before the dark made it difficult to navigate the trail. I took off by myself and walked briskly toward the summit. The trail is well marked and quite steep at times.

Eventually it became clear that I did not have time to reach the top. I turned around and started down so others would not have to wait for me. After several hundred yards, two men joined me and said they were going to the summit and that I could ride home with them after the climb. Two more women joined us and the five of us reached the summit before sunset. We congratulated each other, took some pictures, and I asked each of them to sign my personal journal. Each of us offered our personal prayers and tied small sacramental cloths to tree branches. We were about to leave when several more climbers reached the final steps to the platform on the summit. In all, 21 people were together at the summit of this sacred mountain.

George, an Indian from Washington State, asked us to form a circle. He passed around an eagle feather he had brought from home and each of us offered a prayer in our own way. After we had all offered our prayers, George tied the eagle feather to a tree where it will continue to offer our prayers for many moons. The sun was set when we finished our ritual and several of the others started down the mountain. I stayed back with the last group and when we reached the bottom it was very dark. The sliver of a moon did not cast much light on the dark path.

On the drive back to Rapid City, my partners told me a story that will forever remain a gift in my life. While I was walking up the trail alone, many of the people who had attended my sessions on Appreciative Supervision were visiting about my work and how much they learned. They also said they would not have gone to the summit, except they did not want to leave me out there all alone.

There is a tradition among American Indians and Alaskan Natives to give names to a person after an event or demonstration of some quality. Because of my work with them, and the sharing of the events that evening at Bear Butte, my friends chose the name they would give me. I was moved to tears and my heart felt very full when they shared the name with me. I share it with you, in humility, and the desire to live up to it in my personal and professional life. They called me "He who inspires others to reach the summit."

When someone recognizes in us what we most want to be, we are deeply touched and motivated to live that value even more. One of the best definitions of coaching that I know is, "Inspiring others to reach the summit." The summit of each person's life is as unique as each person.

Supervision is about discovery. It is about discovering the unique journey of each person. I am suggesting a paradigm shift for supervision. Appreciative Supervision is a combination of Appreciative Inquiry and key coaching skills. Appreciative Inquiry is a model for organizational development developed by David Cooperrider and others. It is a strategy for intentional change that identifies the best of "what is" to pursue dreams and the possibilities of "what could be." Appreciative Inquiry is used by organizations to search for the strengths, passions, and life-giving forces found within every system that hold potential for inspired, positive change.

I believe in supervision. I believe supervision is good for both those who give it and those who receive it. As I visit with employees in a variety of organizational settings, I am often struck that supervision is not seen in a very positive light. I ask the question of people: Are you getting the supervision and support you need to do your job in an excellent manner? The responses I receive vary, but a common one is: I know if I do something wrong, I will hear about it. We as leaders owe each other more than that. When we hire a person to work for our organization, we are committing the resources of the company to help that person be a success. Those of us who have the opportunity of supervising another person should recognize it as a sacred honor. We are in a position to provide the attention, resources, and opportunities for these people to evolve into the fine employees they are capable of becoming.

I suggest we need to change our paradigm about supervision. For many people, supervision is about correcting and fixing employees in order to change less than exemplary job performance. With that mindset it is easy to understand why both those who give supervision and receive it do not relish the task. There are other tasks on our job description that actually bring satisfaction, so supervision is put off. Too often it is done only once or twice a year when required for a performance review. It is no wonder that very little real growth happens.

Another issue in the old paradigm of supervision is that exceptional job performance is almost ignored. Why spend time coaching someone who is doing his or her job in an exception manner? Is it not a waste of precious time and energy supervising people who are doing an excellent job? High-performing individuals I visit with tell me they receive little or no attention from their direct supervisor. They will hear about it when they make a mistake or need to improve their work, but under normal routines they receive little consideration from their boss. This old paradigm can be replaced.

Recent research conducted by the Gallop Institute indicates that the single most important factor in job performance and satisfaction is the relationship an employee has with his or her direct supervisor. If I know my direct supervisor believes in me and is committed to my success, I will perform at a higher level and will stay engaged in my organization longer. This is one of the reasons that a new approach to supervision is so needed today. Supervision should be more about appreciation than monitoring. It should be more about recognition than discipline. Supervision should be more about celebrating excellence than identifying and correcting mistakes.

I have been on both ends of supervision. My own experience in organizations has been mixed. There have been times I have received supportive direction from supervisors. I remember these individuals with gratefulness because their support resulted in my personal and professional evolution. There have been other times when I felt ignored by the very person who should have been there coaching me to more effective job performance. I have also been fortunate to supervisor others. This has been one of the most satisfying aspects of my professional life. I always grow when I witness and support excellence in others.

You will receive great satisfaction in watching others perform up to their potential and beyond. You will witness staff exceed even their own expectations. Together we work to identify positive core and signature strengths of the employee. By combining Appreciative Inquiry and coaching skills we can discover stronger relationships resulting in better performance, the result being Appreciative Supervision. Let's look at eight assumptions of Appreciative Inquiry and then at seven key coaching skills.

Eight Assumptions of Appreciative Inquiry

Appreciative Inquiry is an alternative way of looking at organizations and employee performance. It recognizes there is a powerful energy in paying attention to what works. It is being used in many companies these days to build on past strengths to insure future success. The eight assumptions of Appreciative Inquiry provide a clear set of glasses to wear as you partner with other people.

1. In every organization or human being, something works.
2. What we focus on becomes our reality.
3. Reality is created in the moment, and there are multiple realities.
4. Being present to another person influences that person in some way.
5. People have more confidence and comfort to journey to the future (the unknown) when they carry forward part of the past (the known).
6. When we carry parts of the past forward, they should be the best parts.
7. It is important to value and celebrate differences.
8. The language we use creates our reality.

Appreciative Supervision begins with these assumptions and builds a partnership with the employee that adds value to each party as well as the organization. One of the best things we can do for another person is to give them greater clarity about their talents and their potential. It is from this positive core that people grow and become more effective in their work and life. Combining this theory with key coaching skills will significantly enhance the practice of supervision.

Coaching – What It Is and Is Not

Coaching is one of the oldest activities in management. Coaching is a technique that the most effective executives use regularly. Coaching is providing attention, feedback, resources, language, and guidance to another person in order to support their personal and professional growth.

It is important to know what coaching is not. Coaching is not counseling. In a therapeutic relationship, the emphasis is usually on healing or fixing some kind of a problem. Following a traumatic experience, a tragic death or after receiving some life-shattering news, a counselor can help sort out the reality and nurture the process of restoring what was broken or reclaiming a former state of balance. Counseling is helpful when relationships need attention or when an individual is not functioning well. Many organizations provide employee assistance programs for these issues.

Coaching is not about fixing or restoring. It is about development. It provides focus on reality and helps the employee to identify core values, guiding principles, and their root cause for success. Coaching builds on what is working well. This is why all employees are good candidates for coaching.

Too often high-performing individuals do not get the same attention that poor-performing individuals receive. Supervisors do well to provide coaching to all their employees. This would seem strange if coaching and supervision were primarily about fixing what is broken. But since Appreciative Supervision is about growing what is good, it makes sense to provide coaching for outstanding performers. There is value added to both the coach and the employee in the relationship.

Appreciative Supervision Coaching Skills

Here are seven key coaching skills that work together with Appreciative Inquiry to create Appreciative Supervision.

1. **Listening for truth**

   It is important to remember that even if the messages don't immediately make sense to you, your employees are trying to get their needs met in the best way they can. Giving quick answers only reinforces the dependence. Listening helps the employee build self-confidence. Using powerful questions and giving complete attention helps the relationship mature.

2. **Giving messages**

   Identify a *positive* quality, value, or passion the employee exhibits. It is about the employee, not the problem, challenge, or others. Story telling is one of the most fun and most important skills of relating messages. Stories are the way we make sense out of the events of our lives. Stories in books are good. Stories out of our head and our daily experience are even better. Enable employees to see themselves as the heroes of their lives dealing with challenges and opportunities. After listening, you say: *John, you value teamwork and open communication.* That message conveys to the employees that you are listening and you believe them.

3. **Building language skills**

   The language we use creates our reality. Reading and listening build language skills, vocabulary, and self-confidence. One of the goals of coaching is to provide opportunities for the both supervisor and employee to learn language and other literacy skills. Conversation can begin in very simple ways and develop into complex interactions. Learning new words and using them in conversations is an excellent way to do this.

   Using distinctions and evolutionary progressions can be both fun and enlightening. For example, ask your employee: *What is the difference between excellence and perfection? What will evolve your performance from being satisfactory to being significant? Let's talk about this opportunity you brought to me as a problem.* In the response, the employee can identify important factors in job performance in a positive way. In conversations between supervisor and employee, both can better understand the need for professional evolution.

4. Making the employee right and telling the whole truth

Identify employees' blind spots, remind them of their positive core, and tell the truth. If an employee could benefit from your insight, there is a way to share that insight in a way that builds the person up and does not tear down. We have the responsibility to educate each other about the realities of the world. There are tough lessons to learn and we should seek to make learning a positive experience. Use one-on-one conversation when sharing corrective information with an employee. These tough conversations are an important part of supervision. It is in the open dialogue about work that new learnings are discovered. By using Appreciative Supervision, rather than traditional supervision practices, the conversation can happen in a place of strength and courage rather than weakness and vulnerability. In discovering and affirming what works we find the strength to address what does not work.

5. Offering endorsements

Endorsements are words of praise that are true. We cannot spoil adults by giving them too much praise. We want and need to hear compliments. Throughout life, most of us try to win the approval of others. Employees will get attention from us in one way or another. By being pro-active with endorsements, employees will do more of what we recognize as good behavior. By looking for and recognizing outstanding performance, we encourage more of it.

6. Summarizing – "I want for you"

As an executive, it is a joy to share with employees our desires and dreams. We can listen to them, help them identify their intentions, and then inform them that we want the same result. Executives can be champions to their employees, celebrating their ideas about the present and the future. We want our employees to know that we are on their side. We believe in them, sometimes even more than they believe in themselves. We trust them. We want the very best for them. You might say: *John, I know you have expressed a desire for this promotion. That is what I want for you as well. As you meet these three benchmarks it can become a reality.* When you offer this type of summary the employee knows you believe in them and are supporting their personal success.

7. Making requests

It is vital that we offer guidance. There are times when a coach makes specific requests. There is a place for firm guidelines. There is also a place for making requests in order that the employee can make a choice. Our goal is to nurture independent thinkers and mature behaviors. This can only happen as the employee has freedom and the assurance that he or she can make decisions on their own. Make your request a SMART one (Specific, Measurable, Achievable, Relevant and Timed). For example: *I request that you rewrite the guidelines for that project keeping in mind our conversation. I would like to have it back to me one week from today.*

Combining Appreciative Inquiry with coaching skills results in a powerful tool to inspire others to reach their summit. "One Who Inspires Others to Reach the Summit" is a new name all executives can claim as they commit to personal and professional development. You will make a difference in the quality of the community in which you live and lead. Developing a practice of using Appreciative Supervision enhances your effectiveness and adds value to your organization.

Appreciative Supervision Interview Questions

Performance Evaluation

1. Tell of a time in the past six months (or review period) where you felt fully engaged, challenged and appreciated in your work. What were you doing? What were the results? What made it work? Describe the support you received from others.

2. Without being modest, what do you value most about yourself? What do you value most about your work? What do you value most about your organization?

3. In looking at the present and future, what support, training, coaching do you feel would be most helpful for you to perform at an exceptional level?

4. It is next year at this time and you are being recognized for your outstanding performance. Write a brief paragraph about your accomplishments and the reasons you are being recognized.

Personal Development and Balance

1. Describe the balance in your life between personal and professional development. Tell a story about the best things in your life right now.

2. Without being modest, what do you value most about yourself? What do you value most about your primary relationships?

3. As you plan for the next six months what positive behaviors would most enhance your personal and professional development?

4. Write the words your best friend will use to describe you at your funeral or memorial service.

Project Evaluation

1. Describe the best outcomes of the project just completed. Who were the participants and what did each contribute to make it successful? Why did it work?

2. Without being modest, what did you most value about your participation? What did you most appreciate about others' participation?

3. What are three or four key learnings you can claim for future opportunities?

4. It is the year 2010 and your team is being recognized nationally for its outstanding work. Write the headlines and the first paragraph of the article about your work for *Newsweek* magazine.

CHAPTER ELEVEN

Getting to "The Real Conversation" in Business

Jim Peal, PH.D.

WHO IS JIM PEAL?

Jim's reputation as a powerful, master communicator who leads executives and their teams to higher levels of excellence, competence, and productivity is the trademark of his 20-year career. Jim's unique ability to "read" complex situations, formulate and execute an intervention that results in immediate and long-term results is characteristic of his work. Jim's expertise covers three areas:

1. **Keynote workshops**
2. **Executive and team coaching**
3. **Organizational development**

Jim's passion for education, creativity and excellence is demonstrated by his broad educational and work experience. His leadership experience includes serving as CEO of Sage Seminars, Executive Director of Advanced Training Institute, Consultant Manager of the Center for Professional Development, Principal at Management Communication Systems and CEO of the Peal Consulting Group. After completing his undergraduate work at the University of California at Davis, he completed his postgraduate degree at Baylor Medical School and received a doctoral degree from the Union Institute. In addition, Jim is one of the few people certified as an Elite Master Trainer of Neuro-linguistic Programming (NLP).

Companies Jim has worked with include: Levi Strauss, Pfizer, GlaxoSmithKline, Roche, Bristol-Meyers Squibb, Lilly Pharmaceuticals, Amgen, Genentech, Disney, Miramar Systems, Conoco, Lucent, Siemens-Rolm, the University of California, and Restoration Hardware.

Jim Peal, Ph.D.
Oakland, CA • 510-336-0417 • www.peal.com

Jim Peal, PH.D.

Getting to "The Real Conversation" in Business

If you cannot take a stand for someone in your organization, then it is time to have a Real Conversation with that person.

A Real Conversation jump-starts people to action. Sometimes all that is needed is a little jolt to get things moving again. And just like a jump-start, the cables need to be in the right place for the right amount of time. Have you noticed that kicking the tires and cursing a car with a dead battery doesn't make it start? So it is with your judgment and criticism: it will not move anyone in the right direction. You need to take a specific type of action. That is what a Real Conversation is about. It is that spark of your energy that motivates people. A Real Conversation lets people know what they need to do to get back on course. A Real Conversation changes things. It brings greater clarity and a sense of possibility that something new will take place.

What makes a conversation "Real"?

There are three keys to a Real Conversation.

First – you must be *fully present.* It's impossible to have a Real Conversation if your attention is on your blueberry, blackberry or any other "fruit" in your hand. Be fully there with the other person, listening and engaging.

Second – there must be *truth telling.* Everyone knows how to dance around the truth, i.e., beat around the bush. When I'm not having the Real Conversation I know I should be having, I regret the waste of precious mental energy that could be better used getting my Real job done.

Third – a Real Conversation must be a *two-way* conversation. It's not a dump truck, just dumping your thoughts out there on the table and leaving people to deal with them. Real is asking questions. Real is engaging people from the inside out. Real Conversations are motivational.

How do we get to the place where we are fully present, telling the truth, and engaging in a two-way conversation? It seems simple enough, yet these Real Conversations seem to come wrapped in a veil of fear that would have us recoil rather than engage in a meaningful dialog that builds trust.

Consider the following common workplace scenarios:

1. In the last four months John has become obstructive and negative about individual team members and changes in the team.
2. In spite of her expectations, it is unlikely that Janis will be promoted to the director level, because someone who has less tenure is better qualified for the one opening available.
3. Ben has a good performance record and a strong reputation for delivering and getting results. However, his leadership style creates an uncomfortable atmosphere of obedience and silence. His team is afraid to tell him about his negative impact.
4. Your boss has a habit of making innuendos that seem to undermine your authority in front of your team. She seems to be totally unaware of her impact.

What are your first reactions to these scenarios? Do you look forward to dealing with these situations? What are the tough messages that need to be delivered? What needs to be said but has not been spoken? How will you deliver the tough messages?

Are you aware of the Real Conversations that need to happen? Do you make excuses to avoid engaging in a Real Conversation? Do you ignore the Real Conversations hoping that they will simply go away, not realizing that the ensuing silence has a staggering cost to your organization? Approximately 30%-40% of high performers in an organization want Real Conversations with their leader, but do not feel that they can have those conversations. Frustrated high performers are three times as likely to be planning to leave the organization. It does not take a degree in mathematics to calculate the cost of the intellectual horsepower wasted thinking about leaving vs. thinking about contributing to the organization.

Why do these Real Conversations seem to come wrapped in a veil of fear? How do you muster the courage to walk through that fear to reach your goals? This chapter illuminates the way.

Once you walk through the veil, then what? How do you get the issues on the table and navigate your way to success? Blurting it out is one way you can start a Real Conversation. However, there are more elegant, practical ways you can quickly get to the point and make progress.

The top five types of Real Conversations

Figure 1 below shows a useful list of Real Conversation topics to have on your radar screen. Incorporate these topics into ongoing conversations with your people rather than waiting until an annual performance review.

Fig. 1 – The Real Conversation Star

1. Where we are going and commitment to the direction

Communicate goals and direction often. Posting it on your intranet website is nice; but if you want your vision to live inside your people, then it must live inside of you. If you are not authentically inspired by your vision, change it, reword it, or do something so that it is compelling to you. People will follow your energetic lead. Engage your team in creating the direction when appropriate. Remember to explicitly ask them if they understand the stated goals. Ask for their concerns and listen to any concerns or objections they might have. Validate that you have heard their concerns. Better to hear their concerns now than later when more is at risk.

2. **What is expected of me**

   People work best when they know what is expected of them. They are not mind readers, so be very clear. Explain your expectations and then ask what they heard to validate your communication. Outline the consequences of nonperformance at the beginning.

3. **How I am doing**

   Many times people go for years without quality feedback. This is like a compass that does not get proper care—it can get stuck pointing one direction and take the organization off course. Don't expect people to change without input. Give the full spectrum of feedback—what they do well and their opportunities for improvement. One type of feedback without the other is imbalanced. Provide a balanced picture, not just the good stuff or just the bad stuff. Everyone is different; so tailor the message to each person's style.

4. **How I will be developed and advanced**

   People want to know what is in it for them. No one likes to stagnate on the vine. Be proactive when discussing this topic with your people. It is best to have the development conversation prior to their performance review. Let them know the opportunities for development and that you expect them to take an active role in their own development. Financial and other constraints may preclude lavish training programs and opportunities for promotion. It is still important to talk openly about how you will support their growth. Express realistic expectations given the external constraints. Brainstorm about what is possible. Enlist your subordinates in coming up with creative solutions rather than doing it all yourself.

5. How I will be compensated

People don't work just for the money and it is necessary that you have this conversation to complete the picture. Compensation is a key conversation topic to help set expectations. Outline grade level possibilities, the typical milestones that must be reached, and the timeframes for salary and bonus increases. Be clear with them that longevity alone does not justify a pay increase. Many times monetary increases are given across several business units. Be as transparent as possible about the process so that appropriate expectations are set.

Real Conversation best practices checklist

Following are five best practices that make Real Conversations successful.

1. Check your attitude.

Are you assuming that the other person has a negative intent or that you will have a negative outcome? Your mood and attitude play a major part in the outcome of any conversation. Listen to the conversation in your head about the Real Conversation at hand. If it is negative, more than likely you will have a negative outcome. Assuming the other person has negative intentions sets up a defensive situation. If you act defensively, that may cause them to have a similar response.

Most people who work for you don't sit at home and think, "How can I ruin my boss's day? How can I do substandard work?" Usually people are frustrated about something. They are not getting what they need. So check *your* attitude. When someone is callously critical of you, it is harder to respond to what they are saying.... even if they are truly right. Acting self-righteous only makes it harder for them to listen to you and harder to change. Give the benefit of the doubt and give yourself a break from being right about how wrong you think they are.

2. Assume positive intent.

Assume the person is trying to accomplish the stated goals, even though their behavior is not creating a positive impact. Making this shift in thinking creates a positive context. Assuming positive intent transforms your nonverbal signals. Positive intent disallows any self-righteous attitudes and shifts you into a more productive state of mind. Assuming positive intent opens you to the other person's perspective and gives you a sense of where they are coming from. What are their perceptions of you? What are their values/ drivers? What are their concerns and frustrations? Assuming a positive intention on their part helps you be positive and will help create a positive outcome.

3. Build trust and relationships.

Take a sincere interest in people. People can tell when you truly care about them. This can't be faked. When a leader authentically cares for his/her people it instills a deep sense of loyalty. Ask questions to understand their values and drivers. The best way to get to know someone is to ask quality questions and listen fully to the responses. People will respond when you are genuinely curious about them. A few minutes getting to know someone creates currency in the relationship bank that pays dividends later.

Questions to ask: What's important to you at work? What makes that important? What motivates you at work? What de-motivates you?

4. Listen generously.

Listening creates a foundation for credibility and influence. Generous listening means that you are listening with your mind and with your heart as well. Give others your full attention. Give feedback about what you heard and use their words to verify understanding. When you give a person quality attention, they will do the same for you. Having two ears and one mouth means we should listen twice as much as we speak.

5. Prepare ahead of time.

Preparation is essential to a successful Real Conversation. Consider the following steps.

a. Opening: Prepare your opening lines before the discussion. An opening might sound like this: "I'd like to talk with you about

_______ aspect of your performance/how you work/the results you are producing. How is work going for you? How is it being on this team? How do you think you are doing? What would enhance your performance? How can I support you better as your boss? Over the past _____ (#weeks, months) I have noticed an increasing gap between where I think you can perform and where I see you performing. I'm bringing this to your attention now because we are at a threshold where it is a priority that changes are made. I'd like to explain to you what I have been noticing then hear from you about how you see your performance and what you think you can do to close the gap."

b. Frame: Decide how you will frame the issues: "The issue(s) is (are)…", "An example is….", "This is the change I would like to see…."

c. Bring nonverbals into the discussion: Pay attention to nonverbal behavior and respond verbally to it. If they frown or furrow their brow, stop right there and ask, "Something just shifted, do you have a question? Or can I re-explain something?" Or, "It looks like I may have touched a nerve." Or, "It seems that perhaps you are not understanding my intentions." Stop and self-correct as you go along. Don't let nonverbal signals go unnoticed. Bring them into the conversation.

d. Check for understanding: "What did you hear me say?" "How does it impact you?" "What questions/concerns do you have?"

e. Play through a couple of scenarios: How do you think they will respond? Best case? Worst? What could come up? How would you handle it?

f. Establish a plan: "How do you think we should move forward?" "What will you do? How can I support you?" "When will you follow-up? What will that look like?" or "This is when we will meet and what our meeting will look like."

g. Close: Consider how you will close the conversation. "We've covered a lot of ground. Thank you for your participation. I am looking forward to working on these issues."

Worst practices

There are a few things that you can do that will create a negative trajectory for your Real Conversations.

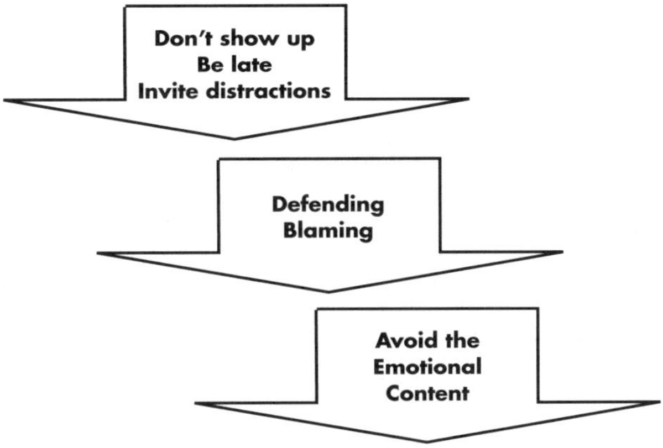

Fig. 2 – Worst Practices

1. Be absent without notice, be late or invite distractions – These behaviors send a clear message that the other person is not important.
2. Defending and blaming – Theses two behaviors are the cornerstones for drama to take place. Being defensive sends a signal that you are not interested in hearing what the other person has to say. As a leader you must model the behaviors you want to see from others. If something goes wrong ask yourself: What did you learn? What will you do differently next time? How can you pass on this learning to others rather than just pointing out what went wrong?
3. Avoiding the emotional content – Passionate people bring their emotions to work. If someone is upset, assuming positive intent means that you take the stance: People don't get upset unless something is important. So if someone is upset, witness and guide them through it. You can say, "I can see that this is important to you." Ask them if they need a break. Often emotions just need acknowledgement and space and they will clear up.

Wrap up

There are three keys to a Real Conversation: be fully present, tell the truth, and engage in a two-way conversation. The five real conversations are: Direction & Commitment, What's expected, How I am doing, Growth and Development, and Compensation. Use your Real Conversation checklist: check your attitude, assume positive intent, build trust and relationships, listen generously, and prepare ahead of time.

Do it!

If you *cannot* take a stand for someone in your organization, then you need to have a Real Conversation with that person. Most of us need a jolt to take action because we shy away from looking at the actual costs of inaction in our relationships and in our life's work. Our inner self knows that much has gone unspoken and ultimately wants to operate from that deeper truth and openness.

Use these tips as a jump-start to stimulate trust and partnerships through conversation. Move out of the comfort zone of your excuses and take action. Take the risk to achieve a positive result. Each and every moment presents you with a new opportunity to engage in a Real Conversation. Grab hold, feel the juice, and be courageous or remain passive, disengaged and uninspiring. The choice is yours.

Getting to the Real Conversations – Coaching Questions

1. What topics do you avoid in your business conversations?

____

____

2. What stops you from having these Real Conversations?

____

____

3. What is the risk for you personally?

____

____

4. What does it cost you/your organization to avoid these topics?
   a. Energy level
   b. Performance and productivity
   c. Attitude and morale
   d. Self-concept
   e. Health
   f. Carryover to other relationships

5. With whom do you need to have a real conversation? List their names and topics.

____

____

6. What verbal and nonverbal signals do you send out that communicate that it is not OK to approach you?

____

____

7. What is your preferred way to receive feedback? Have you communicated your feedback style to your boss, peers, and staff?

____

____

8. What action will you take? When?

____

____

CHAPTER TWELVE

We Need to Talk: The Employee Feedback Survival Guide

Kate Zabriskie

Kate Zabriskie is a high-energy, high-impact, speaker and trainer. She founded Business Training Works, a soft-skills training company, to answer a need in the marketplace for affordable, relevant, fast-paced, business training.

Based just outside of Washington, D.C., she and her team have trained for corporations, nonprofits, foundations, government agencies, associations, colleges, and schools throughout the United States. Some of her clients include Bank One, Schering Plough, The United States Coast Guard, Microsoft, Fitch Ratings, and The University of Maryland.

Kate cut her teeth in the training business working with Padgett Thompson and National Seminars Group. As a trainer, speaker, and business coach, she is known for her engaging, energetic style, sense of humor, and ability to make learning fun. She specializes in soft-skills training: from real-world business etiquette to power presentation skills.

Kate brings over fourteen years of solid business experience to her programs. After graduating from George Mason University, she began her career as a trade show exhibits manager for a national defense association. Upon completing her MBA at the University of Texas, she joined Andersen Consulting, working with a diverse client base. In 1996, Kate was recruited by the Franklin Mint, where her responsibilities included art and video licensing, new product development, and human resources training.

Kate's diverse background is the foundation for her work in soft-skills business training, coaching, and speaking. Her understanding of multiple industries and appreciation of different work cultures help her to guide people where they want to go and improve their business skills.

Business Training Works, Inc.
Port Tobacco, MD • 301-934-3250 • www.businesstrainingworks.com

Kate Zabriskie

We Need to Talk: The Employee Feedback Survival Guide

I really need to talk to him. I really need to let her know how she's doing. Sound familiar? As managers, thoughts such as those may run through your mind daily when you think about the people you supervise.

Unfortunately and all too often, many of us don't seize the opportunities to give performance feedback other than during an annual review. Of course we have our excuses. I don't have time. He already knows he's doing a great job. I don't want to hurt her feelings. The list goes on.

Not giving solid feedback is a key ingredient in the recipe for employee failure and your failure as a manager. On the other hand, knowing how to effectively communicate your expectations and evaluations of employee performance can set you apart from the mediocre and advance your career.

The information in this chapter will help you to avoid common feedback mistakes, establish a feedback process, discover your strengths and weaknesses, and lay out a template for coaching and counseling conversations.

Getting Started

Take a moment and review the employee statements below. How do you think the supervisors could improve each situation?

I work for someone who only points out what I do wrong. He never recognizes what I do well. It is so frustrating. I feel so deflated every time he talks to me. The amazing thing is, my performance evaluations are good and he tells other people that I'm doing a good job. - Greg

I always get positive feedback from my boss. She says, "Great job!" and other nice things to me. The problem is that I feel stuck. I have asked what I need to do better to grow and I get nothing but more general comments. I'm thinking of leaving to work somewhere else. - Roger

I never know how I'm doing until I get my performance evaluation. My boss talks to me randomly. We never have a scheduled meeting together. I'm starting to wonder if he knows how to manage people. - Jean

My boss yelled at me in front of our whole office. She said that she had never worked with anyone so stupid. The next day, she acted as if it never happened. This is the second time she's done something like this. I don't know how she keeps her job. - Lee

If you decided that those supervisors are in trouble, you're right. Greg, Roger, Jean, and Lee have one thing in common for sure: managers who don't manage. Like plants, people need care and feeding to grow. If they don't know what they are doing well and what they need to do to improve, they can hardly develop as employees.

Self Evaluation

Before we address those supervisors' problems, consider some of your own behaviors. Evaluate the statements below, and rate yourself against each using the following scale (1) Always, (2) Most of the Time, (3) About Half of the Time, (4) Some of the Time, (5) Never.

1. In both formal and informal feedback, I usually focus on what my direct reports do poorly, not what they do well. 1 2 3 4 5

2. I rarely use examples to highlight their good or bad behaviors when I have feedback discussions. 1 2 3 4 5

3. I often wait until a situation gets really bad before I deal with it. 1 2 3 4 5

4. I usually make my own boss the bad guy when I give negative feedback. 1 2 3 4 5
5. On occasion I have given negative feedback in public. 1 2 3 4 5
6. I rarely follow up after I have given feedback to an employee. 1 2 3 4 5
7. I often give negative feedback via email. It's easier. 1 2 3 4 5
8. I don't believe in schedules. Rarely do I have a scheduled face-to-face discussion. 1 2 3 4 5
9. I don't worry about developing people for the next step. We have enough to do as it is. 1 2 3 4 5
10. When an employee messes up, there is little hope for improvement. Therefore I don't spend much time on trying to change their behaviors. I wait for them to quit or fire them. 1 2 3 4 5

Total your score: ___________

Score of 10 – 20: You have several areas that require improvement.
Score of 21 – 30: You have some areas that require improvement.
Score of 31 – 40: You manage the feedback process fairly well. Focus on bringing up your lower scores.
Score of 41 – 50: You manage the feedback process well. Continue to keep lines of communication open with those who report to you.

Thinking back to Greg, Roger, Jean, and Lee, there is some hope for their managers. Consider these approaches:

Greg's supervisor needs to praise Greg's good work in addition to pointing out his improvement areas.

Roger's boss needs to think about getting Roger to the next level. If there are roadblocks, they need to be discussed. If there is no "next level," cross training should be considered.

Jean's manager needs to prepare for and schedule weekly face-to-face meetings. Random popping in takes away from his credibility.

Lee's supervisor needs to apologize for her previous actions and commit to more professional behavior. She and Lee need to start at the beginning and discuss their expectations of each other. It could take several months for Lee's supervisor to regain her lost credibility.

Feedback Conversation Roadmap

At this point you have had a chance to review some management mistakes and taken a quick assessment quiz in regard to your own feedback style. Now we will look at two conversation models for feedback. The first is to improve poor performance. The second is to encourage strong performance.

There are many ways to give feedback to an employee about poor performance. However, regardless of style, the objective this type of feedback session should be to change counterproductive behavior(s).

Before talking to someone about a work behavior you find disturbing, it is important that you do your homework. To prepare, review and consider each of the following eight questions.

1. Does the person understand what his or her job is? How do you know?
2. Does the person fully understand your expectations in terms of quality and quantity of work? Expected attitude? Professional behavior? How do you know?
3. Has the person performed up to your expectations in the past? If yes, what do you think has caused the dip in performance?
4. Have the organization's expectations recently changed?
5. Does the person have the skill and ability to do the job?
6. Is the person overqualified? Under-qualified?
7. Does the person know that there is a problem?
8. Are you or others in the organization contributing to the problem?

Once you have those answers, you are one step closer to addressing the problem. Without going through this exercise, you may find that you are addressing the wrong issue and/or person.

General Rules to Consider

In order to promote a positive reaction to your feedback, here are several guidelines you should follow:

- Give feedback in private.
- Make sure that you and the other person are not angry.
- Comment on the behavior, not the person.
- Use examples.
- Ask questions for understanding.
- Follow up.

Sample Improvement Feedback Session

Once you have prepared and practiced what you plan to say, you may find the delivery relatively easy. And although every situation is unique, planning is universal. Take a look at the sample script below. It is a blueprint for a formal feedback session about changing negative behavior—in this case, a situation where an employee contributes inappropriately in meetings.

1. **Identify the behavior that concerns you.**

   In this afternoon's staff meeting, when the boss asked about the latest test scores, you started speaking just as I was about to respond.

2. **State why the behavior just mentioned is a problem.**

   I could tell by the reaction from the boss' face that she, too, was surprised that you answered the question and not me.

3. **Describe how you felt about the behavior and why it is a problem.**

   I found this upsetting for several reasons. First, the numbers you gave were not the latest available. Second, we did not present a unified front. That made us both look bad.

4. **Ask questions to confirm their perception.**

   Do you understand why I found this frustrating? Why did you speak up so quickly?

   [Note: It is very important that you not skip this step. You may find out information that you did not know. For instance, "I spoke because that's what you told me to do when we met on Tuesday." Oops, you've now got a different problem on your hands.]

5. **State the desired new behavior.**

   Unless we plan otherwise, I would like to be the one to do the reporting for our group. I will look for ways to include you in the presentations where appropriate.

6. **Describe what will happen if the new behavior is not used.**

   If this kind of thing happens again, we will have to revisit the attendance list for the staff meeting.
   [Note: Depending on the situation, you may want to skip this step. If it is a first time occurrence, this step might be overkill.]

7. **Get agreement.**

   Can we agree that this is the way we will handle reporting in the future?

8. **State a positive.**

   This is the first time anything like this has ever happened. You have always worked hard and been dedicated to the organization. I appreciate your enthusiasm. I am sure that this is not going to be a recurring event.

9. **Close.**

   Do you have any questions? If not, then we can get back to work.

10. **Document the session.**

    [Note: Always document your conversations. This should not be too difficult since you are going to write out what you will say ahead of time anyway.]

11. **Follow up at the next appropriate time.**

    (During the next face-to-face after the next staff meeting…)
    I wanted to let you know that I thought today's staff meeting went well. Thank you for waiting for me to ask you to present your information. I believe that we presented a unified front and worked well as a team.

Additional Tips to Consider

- Depending on the situation, your style, the style of the employee, etc., your tone may change. It is important, however, that you remain professional and non-accusatory.
- If you are dealing with an employee who gets emotional, do not let that throw you. Continue with your conversation. It might also help to have some tissues on hand.
- Your preparation time should be about 30 minutes. If you prepare well, the conversation in most cases will not last more than 15 minutes.
- Do not allow the employee to take you off track or to bring up the behavior of others. If that happens, simply state, "I understand what you are telling me, but right now we are talking about your behavior."
- Write out your notes in longhand and in bullet format. Most likely you will reference the bullets. However, if you get stuck, you can read from your longhand. For best results, be sure to use a conversational tone when writing.
- Give the employee a chance to succeed after having the conversation. If you expect the worst, you will probably get it.

Supervisor Beware! Don't Fall into the Enabling Zone

Even after an initial feedback session, you might find that although you are not directly causing employee behavioral problems, you are enabling them to exist. Be honest: are your actions allowing an employee to exhibit unproductive, disruptive, or destructive behavior in your organization? Review the statements below. Place a mark next to those that accurately reflect your behavior over the last four weeks.

__ I avoided an employee who I feel is a problem.

__ I spent my commute time and my time at home worrying about a problem employee.

__ I allowed an employee to share extensive details about his/her personal life with me.

__ I did not convey concerns I have about an employee to my supervisor.

__ I made excuses for an employee.

__ I did not verify an employee's far-fetched story.

__ I allowed an employee to be rude to me or to others.

__ I asked other employees to tolerate another employee's unprofessional behavior.

__ I allowed my compassion for an employee's personal struggles to interfere with getting the work done.

__ I said yes when I wanted to say no.

__ I tried to solve an employee's personal problem.

__ I accepted substandard work with no comment.

__ I overlooked unprofessional behavior.

__ I overlooked unethical behavior.

__ I was more concerned about being liked than being respected.

If you checked any of the statements above, you may be contributing to the problem. If that is the case, you must self monitor better and avoid such actions. It is critical that you set, demonstrate, and expect a professional standard of behavior from yourself and those you supervise.

Other Roadblocks

In addition to enabling behavior, you may encounter some other roadblocks. Below are potential problems as well as their solutions.

Problem: I've never enforced behaviors in the past. How can I start now?
Solution: You must start fresh with an employee. Meet with them and explain that you are entering a new phase and that you and he/she need to talk about expectations. Briefly apologize for any errors you have made in the past and move on. Set weekly meetings and prepare for them. It will take several months for the new you to become the norm.

Problem: I have not demonstrated the behaviors I expect.
Solution: Start exhibiting those behaviors without fail, and then see the previous answer.

Problem: I feel sorry for the employee. His/her home life is horrible.
Solution: Separate yourself from the employee's personal problems. Your focus should be on work. Not doing so will potentially complicate your working relationship. Furthermore, if you supervise several people, the others will come to resent your favoritism.

Problem: I simply hate conflict. Telling someone that they need to change is just too hard.
Solution: Practice. Realize that in the long run you are actually holding the person back. Remember, your goal is to help them succeed. If you let substandard behavior occur, are you really helping the employee?

Helping employees to succeed is an important part of your job. Fortunately, not all conversations will be the negative kind. In fact, most should be positive. The good news about that is that the more you interact with those you supervise, the easier both kinds of conversations will become.

Sample Positive Feedback Session

If you are like most supervisors, you will have many more opportunities to praise rather than criticize. Actually taking the time to give that praise is essential to developing the best in those you supervise.

1. Identify the behavior that you wish to praise.

I wanted to let you know that I thought the meeting with the client went extremely well. You did a terrific job of fielding their questions.

2. Describe how the behavior benefits the organization.

Servicing the client well is a big part of our job and I thought your efforts today contributed to our achieving that goal.

3. Ask about "next step" needs.

Is there anything you need from me so that you can put the proposal together? I would like to review it within the next few weeks.

4. Ask about developmental needs.

Eventually I would like you to be able to meet with clients without me. In addition to shadowing me for the next few months, what else can I do to help you continue to grow your skill set?

Notice how both feedback session examples comment on behaviors. Whether you like the employee personally should have little impact on how you manage him or her. Successful management is less about liking and more about respecting people and growing their abilities.

The Least You Need to Know

As you might have concluded by now, successful feedback is consistent and fair communication about work. The more you do it, the easier it becomes. Remember —

1. Your success depends on the success of those who work for you.
2. Liking an employee is not the same thing as coaching an employee.
3. Preparation is critical. Management on the fly is not usually effective.

Successful management is work. By using the suggestions and templates in this guide, you should be well on your way to helping those around deliver top performances—ultimately enhancing the success of your own career!

POWER TOOLS

SECTION III

Tools for High Impact Leadership

CHAPTER THIRTEEN

Choices and Connections for Executive Success

Karen L. Anderson, M.A., CTD

Author and professional speaker, Karen L. Anderson investigates what makes people do what they do. She is also fascinated by how ethical, empathetic leaders influence and inspire others to do what the leader wants.

After three decades of professional and community service in roles that include being a department leader, a corporate trainer and consultant, an adjunct professor, a civil mediator, a certified trainer and developer, a construction manager, and a business owner, Karen is still baffled by human behavior. Her insights will entertain and encourage you in your pursuit of happiness and freedom of expression.

Karen's clients include the Environmental Protection Agency, the United Way, Honeywell, Meals on Wheels, Sprint, national professional associations, universities, and individuals seeking self-development. She has shared and exchanged learning with thousands of seminar participants and students.

Karen's mission in life is to help others transform communication skills into persuasive strategies for creating positive choices and connections in the world. Karen will be pleased if your world as you know it—and your relationships as you live them—improve as a result of her experiences and expertise.

Anderson Catalyst Training Services
Lenexa, KS • 866-240-3935 • www.acts-ion.com

Karen L. Anderson, M.A., CTD

Choices and Connections for Executive Success

Our choices and our connections determine our success. Two strategic actions will improve a new executive's chances for fulfillment on the job: overriding fear and creating relationships. This chapter contains tips, tools, and techniques for positive and productive initiation into the leadership ranks.

Psychologists are social scientists who seek the reasons why people do what they do, believe what they believe, and think what they think. They identify pain, fear, and want as the three primary motivators—our internal drivers for doing what we do or for not doing what we could do. The second of those is the most intriguing and debilitating. Fear is the epitome of uncertainty, insecurity, worry, and anxiety. Fear can permeate a creative brain and disintegrate a brilliant plan. In Part I we will investigate two major fear factors that can cripple a newly launched executive career and what to do to override them.

Psychologists also define personality traits as those preferred or typical behaviors and thinking patterns an individual is most likely to demonstrate. How can we identify safe and effective guidelines for interacting within a diverse workplace? In Part II we will investigate four ways to make connections with the people positioned around the new executive.

Part I: Choices

I was headed off to St. Louis for college. I was unsure of arriving in an unfamiliar airport and anxious about arranging ground transportation to the campus. My dad seemed impatient with me. He expected that I would act like an independent adult, not a scared teenager of 17. I decided then that if he thought I could go out on my own, that I would manage somehow. Although I did not overcome my fear of being alone in an unknown world, I did decide to override the fear. I want to believe that my dad is proud of his independent daughter who now speaks up and speaks out confidently as she travels the United States from airport to airport.

Fears surround us, ambush us, elude us, unravel us, and confound us. Fears such as failure, risk, and rejection have a negative nature. Others such as success, responsibility, and commitment have a positive nature. The truth is, however, that fear is neutral. How you respond to it is what makes it negative or positive. Simply put, you choose to accept or reject fear. You choose to be paralyzed or empowered by fear. You override fear by making a decision and living with the consequences.

Fear of Failure, Risk, and Rejection

The first fear factors to consider are **fear of failure, risk, and rejection.** These fears can hold us in custody like we were awaiting trial for an offense we have not yet committed. We allow disappointment and perfectionism to command our inaction. Haven't we all been disappointed in our own performance at sometime in the past? Haven't we all seen others fall on their faces and heard the critical remarks others have made about their incompetent performance? Who in their right mind would want to make a fool of themselves?

Leaders do! To be a leader requires risking failure—taking the chance of being imperfect. Experience and expertise evolve from such vulnerability. After learning what does not work, we can narrow the gap to find what does work. Thomas Edison taught himself thousands of ways how not to the build a light bulb before he found the way to accomplish his dream. All inventors, innovators, and leaders run into similar circumstances where determination becomes the deciding factor in differentiating themselves.

Fear of risk includes fear of failure and more. Failure is a product, whereas risk is the process that results in failure—or success. Steve Jobs, of Apple, NeXT, and Pixar, has experienced both failure and success. He explained to the graduates at Stanford University that facing death from cancer convinced him life is worth living: "Your time is limited, so don't waste it living someone else's life.... Don't let the noise of others' opinions drown out your own inner voice. Most important, have the courage to follow your heart and intuition." Some of his audience will be executives within the decade.

An effective executive must possess an entrepreneurial spirit. Entrepreneurs operate in the world of informed risk. They challenge business rules every time they launch a product or sell an idea. Rather than resisting change, these creative people embrace it. Rather than playing it safe, they simply play it out. This means testing your decisions. It means reconsidering decisions when additional information comes to light. Redesigning and reframing make up the daily landscape of an entrepreneur like Jobs.

Years ago as a single mom, I realized I needed a business degree in addition to my master's in education. I needed to be more marketable than I was. I wanted to support my children and purchase a home someday. A teacher's salary was not enough. Should I take the risk? I told my dad how discouraged I was. "It'll take five years of night school after working all day" I said. He asked how old I would be in five years, and then added, "Wouldn't you rather be 40 with a degree, than 40 without one?" No more complaining. Step out and take the risk.

Psychologist Abraham Maslow observed how people make decisions. His Hierarchy of Human Needs model tells us about the fear of rejection. He claimed that once a person has essentials such as shelter, clothing, food, water, and safety, that person's next need is "belongingness" with a social group or community. We all want to belong—to be included, not excluded. Litigation abounds over diversity and dignity in the workplace. We ask, "Treat me with respect, even though you may not respect my ideas and actions." Maintain dignity for others and you will gain their respect.

People feel rejected when their successes are ignored and their failures are amplified. Too often people are recognized for what they *do not* do well, rather than being recognized for what they *do* well. The number one complaint in America among adult workers is lack of positive recognition. Take note and recognize people for a task well done.

Abby Olson, of Olson & Associates, concurs that affirmations and dignity are significant issues in the workplace. She advises us to discourage negativity, avoid favoritism, and "make wine out of the office grapevine." Abby knows how to make people feel included and valued. She says we should:

1. Ask permission: "May I do this for you now?" People want to know that their preferences and ideas matter.

2. Offer choices: "Would you like to meet this afternoon or tomorrow morning?" Adults want some control over their lives, jobs, and schedules. Give them small choices, especially when big decisions are not up for discussion.

3. Give explanations: "I made this decision for the following reasons..." Although you need not be on the defensive, you do want others to comply. If you want them to comply, tell them why. It is a sign of respect. People will usually go along with your direction, despite their disagreement or lack of commitment. They do it to please you. Consequently, you should make decisions that withstand the test of time and explanation. Here are two tips to provide insight for you in decision making:

   A. When faced with a decision, most of us begin with the optional courses of action that spring to mind. A better way is to begin with examining the criteria by which you will gauge the quality of the alternatives.

   B. Many people badger themselves about procrastinating. The distinction between procrastination and preparation is significant. Prior to a decision, you are in the preparation stage. This takes varying amounts of time as you gather and consider information. After making a decision, you enter the procrastination stage – the time between planning and implementation of a decision. If procrastination lasts too long, consider what factors are causing it: Was a decision maker absent from the decision selection? Are there people who have not committed to the decision? Is the timing not quite right? There *is* a reason for the procrastination. Identify it. Be clear about how you make decisions and take action.

After my grandma died, my sisters found a yellowed newspaper clipping of a Boy Scout who saved ten people from sure death in a fire. The article spoke of a heroic 13-year old who insisted they could all save their lives by jumping from a third-floor window. To prove it, he jumped first. From the ground he coaxed them all to safety. My dad had never spoken of this horrible choice until we asked him if he broke any bones in the jump. Sometimes you have to decide to jump even though you might break a bone or two. Pay attention to both the preparation and the procrastination stages.

Fear of Success, Responsibility, and Commitment

The **fear of success**, **responsibility**, and **commitment** is another opportunity for making choices. Success keeps company with competence, confidence, and conscience. Competence suggests knowledge, skill, and the ability to perform a job according to standards and expectations. Confidence is based on experience and belief in oneself or team. Conscience is doing what is right within the context of relationships and values. The unethical episodes at Enron and other corporate fiascos prove that the element of conscience must be blended with competence and confidence to ensure long-term success.

So the question is, how does one overcome the fear of success? Affirmations are one technique. Affirmations provide positive self-talk that help you visualize and materialize success. Using affirmations for yourself and your employees can be beneficial in surprising ways. Use positive and productive words. Avoid *no*, *not*, and *never*. Say, "I am an effective executive" and your brain will believe that you are. Furthermore, your brain will help you make it true by alerting you to ways you can become even more effective. Have you ever experienced a time when you wished for something and then it came true? When you say an affirmation aloud and write it down as a reminder, you progress toward that ideal characteristic. You see and hear opportunities that you would not have noticed without the affirmation.

Also, use affirmations for encouraging others. Say, "Do your best. I trust your judgment and skill. Let me know if I can assist you by removing obstacles or providing resources." Positive thinking builds both community and productivity.

You can help others be successful through honest feedback. Recently, *Fortune* magazine reported that the number one reason for manager failure was not dealing with poor performers. Use these guidelines from Amy Bloom, novelist and contributor to *O* Magazine, to deliver the truth in feedback:

Guidelines for Telling the Truth:

1. Is it kind?
2. Is it true?
3. Is it useful?

Truthful feedback requires firm, gentle, and clear communication of your expectations, timelines, and consequences. The emphasis should always be on positive, desired results, not perfectionism or punishment.

Remember in giving feedback that perfect careers, perfect projects, and perfect people do not exist. Perfect moments do, however. Enjoy them! Great leaders know this. When the PowerPoint presentation suffers an electronic glitch, recognize the humor of the situation. A perfect laugh energizes everyone and creates a context in which to invite and absorb pertinent content in later moments.

How do you celebrate success? Suzy Makalous recommends "putting fun to work" by using whimsical props and throwing spontaneous parties with bubbles and poppers—anything to celebrate the moment and recognize accomplishments. According to Suzy, increased employee retention and morale result from sharing fun. She recommends celebrating partial successes as well as complete ones. Reward both individual and team goals. Reward people with positive recognition and affirmation—and do the same for yourself.

That leads us to overcoming the fear of responsibility. By celebrating your own small successes, you become more comfortable with the larger ones. Taking on small responsibilities leads to becoming more comfortable with the greater ones. Ted Findlay of The Findlay Group identified ten job responsibilities for every employee, no matter the job title or job description.

Ten Job Responsibilities:

1. Be on time.
2. Be present—mentally and physically.
3. Act like a professional. Be credible, dependable, and accessible. Keep your promises and others' confidences.
4. Be productive. Look busy and *be* busy.
5. Produce quality work. This is your signature.
6. Meet target dates. Negotiate early when you know a deadline is unrealistic.
7. Communicate well and often.
8. Learn constantly. Professional development is essential to remaining marketable.

9. Control expense and waste. Recycle resources, work efficiently, and cut costs.
10. Be safety minded. The average Worker's Compensation claim costs an employer $7,000 for females and $9,000 for males. Humans are not expendable.

Override your fear of responsibility by taking small, manageable steps toward being accountable for yourself and the role you play in the organization. Hold yourself and your employees accountable for their behavior, decisions, and actions. Create a culture of fairness through your consistent modeling of these ten responsibilities. It demonstrates your commitment to the team and the organization.

The fear of commitment has been the brunt of bad dating jokes for decades. It is true, however, that there is a sense of eternity in the promise to "be there." Leonard Sweet, theologian and writer, remembers sitting on the bench during school team sports. His experience applies to business. He says people fear commitment because they have been sitting on the bench too long. How can you get your employees and co-workers off the bench and into the game? Find ways to involve them and encourage commitment. Ask them to participate and contribute. Your commitment will grow as you include them, listen to them, and affirm them. Also, learn to recognize the stages of bench warming.

Four Stages of Bench Warming:

1. I could do it better. When we are not involved, we will never be committed. We observe and criticize co-workers' performance.
2. The coach is incompetent. We criticize the supervisor's ability because the supervisor is apparently not smart enough to use us.
3. I hope someone gets injured. If someone gets hurt or sick, at least we can play part of the game.
4. I hope we lose. As long as we are not encouraged to make a contribution, we do not care if our competition wins and we lose.

Clearly, the lesson is to get people involved and keep them engaged. In return they are apt to reward us with their loyalty and commitment to the team and organization.

Fear of commitment can also cause us to miss our goals. As a young student, I ran for president of my class. I lost by one vote. My dad regretted that I had not believed in myself enough to vote for myself. I thought I was being polite by voting for my opponent. My dad said I did not deserve the office if I did not commit to it with my vote. Lack of commitment is a sure way to sabotage a career.

Managing Fear

So what must we do to manage fear? Take these three steps:

1. Face it!
2. Name it!
3. Override it!

We must know what we are facing, what causes it, and what we can do about it. Denying or avoiding fear does not make it go away. But, making the choice to go through it leads to increased competence, confidence, and conscience for the advancing executive.

Part II: Connections

Recently, a business associate asked me what universal truths exist for leading groups with diverse personalities. My colleague mentioned how many professional training programs incorporate personality profiles into the mix for professional and executive skills.

Four relational connections—communication, negotiation, management, and teamwork—are critical to leading work groups today and apply equally to all personality types. To manage others we may use our positional power, the authority we are given because of our job. Yet, to connect with one another, we must risk vulnerability and use the personal power that has nothing to do with our job.

A fellow Navy pilot in my dad's squadron told me that he would fly anywhere my dad asked, even forty years after their last flight together. Dr. Ed Belinski said my dad led through personal power, not rank. My dad said one time in his military career, he did use his positional power to keep a young suicidal pilot grounded. Later the young pilot went over the Skipper's head. I remember making the visit with my mom to the widow and her three children. We are each responsible for our choices and how we choose to connect with those around us. People will esteem you for conducting business using your personal power. Use your positional (job) power as a last resort.

How can an executive become an inspiration to others? How do you make those relational connections? First, consider communication as a relational connection. Effective communication skills are basic to success. We all want others to talk with us, to be direct with us, and to value our input. Three communication behaviors we appreciate from our leaders and co-workers are listening without interrupting, asking permission regarding our time and space, and expressing empathy for our emotional well-being.

Second, good negotiation skills create a respectful atmosphere in which to work and connect. Negotiation skills are extensions of basic communication skills. We all appreciate it when leaders and co-workers are committed to finding commonalities and similarities, honoring fairness through consistent and dignified treatment, and giving forgiveness in the face of unintentional frailty or fault. Leading a team, a company, or a nation requires refined negotiation skills.

Third, management skills provide a necessary framework in which leaders and co-workers can offer encouragement, accept responsibility, and nurture accountability. When leaders and co-workers are convinced of one another's competence, even when our personal confidence waivers, we can rise to the task at hand. Performance and productivity improve when we have the support and resources from others around us. Karen Martley, with the Center for Business and Technology, eloquently clarifies the word empowerment: "Empowerment is not abandonment." A good manager remains accessible for consultation and resources. A good manager gives encouragement and feedback.

Finally, teamwork evolves through sharing credit, showing recognition, and developing trust. Team leaders and team members bond over time and through stressful conditions by carrying the load, jumping the hurdles, and earning the trophies together. If not *with* all, then always *for* all of the team!

We hunger for personal connection within the automated and technical workplace. Being treated as a valuable and valued person within the organization encourages each of us to be a loyal manager, employee, team member, customer, or partner. Betsy Kay, an executive risk manager for the Williams Companies, remembers her early years there: "I could see the task, but not the people. It's a people world." She learned to address people issues in order to accomplish the tasks on her agenda. Begin today to connect with the people around you.

Conclusion

Fear is a powerful motivator. Whether the fears are perceived as negative or positive, we have our personal power and positional power to help us override those fears. Whether we allow our fears to rule us, or we rule our fears makes a difference in the quality of our relationships with those around us. Our choices and our ability to create connections with others determine the overall success of our careers.

Our choices and our connections are about our decisions and their consequences. To live the life and create the career we were meant to have requires that we employ our personal power without abusing our positional power. My dad would coach you to travel into unfamiliar airports, get more education, vote for yourself, and avoid pulling rank. I also believe Cdr. Charles R. Anderson, USN Ret., would recommend the following:

> Make decisions that have consequences you want to live with and make connections that create relationships that you want to work among. You create your own career.

Dedicated to Cdr. Charles R. Anderson, USN Ret.

The best leader a squadron, a business, or a family could ever have.

CHAPTER FOURTEEN

The Big Three: Focus, Execution & Me

Charles A. Breeding

Do you sometimes feel that you lose your focus? Is the *execution* of objectives and goals gaining higher and higher priority in your world?

"I'm not the Sage on the Stage … just the Guide on the side."

When asked, "What type of work do you do?" his reply is, "I'm in the *life-changing* business." Charlie Breeding has been working with executives and managers, coaching their improved performance, facilitating executive retreats, delighting audiences, and training and consulting with clients for over 22 years.

Since 1994, PI^2 has partnered with a handful of clients in pervasive, long-term performance improvement projects and services at the organizational and personal levels to *institute performance improvement.*

Working with organizations in twenty-five industries, the public sector, small- and medium-sized companies and private institutions, Charlie has distilled an integrated model of increased leadership effectiveness and organizational performance yielding demonstrated, proven returns on investment and impact.

Like Moses learned the hard way, one has to learn to *"let go" intelligently. LET GO Leadership* is about duplicating oneself by delegating, deputizing and leading in a specific, particular manner. Can you duplicate or replicate yourself? Can you build a culture of *execution excellence*? Master three things and master your life and life's work. Read on…

Performance Improvement Institute
Belews Creek, NC • 336.643.1115 • www.ccfs.biz

Charles A. Breeding

The Big Three: Focus, Execution & Me

What is your central *focus* today? How well do you consistently *execute* on that focus? How do *you* need to change and adapt in order to ***focus*** and ***execute*** and ***lead*** more effectively? Whether you are an executive, executive coach, a consultant or aspiring to be one, mastering the three key behaviors of performance will set you above the rest with illuminating leadership and improved communication—like light in a dimly lit room.

These three areas of personal mastery—focus, execution, and leadership—will pay the greatest dividends for the time invested. With them, you'll lead effectively at the highest levels. Without them, your execution excellence potential and consistency is severely limited regardless of your role or station in life.

Consider that as people we are either "green and growing" or "ripe and rotting" in our personal and professional development. Think about it. I've observed in my 27 years of work that the people who *need* training and performance improvement the most want it the *least*; and the people who need training the least want it the *most*. The fact that you're reading this book is testimony to that fact—you're looking for a competitive edge.

Entropy: Your Constant Enemy

Do you recognize the constant need to deal with ambiguity, chaos and confusion? Everyone is fighting one devil constantly—entropy. Entropy is the second law of thermodynamics and essentially states that in nature, everything goes from a state of order to a state of disorder—naturally, by itself. In other words, at this very moment dust is settling everywhere around you. Right now, your car is losing its value. Mechanically it is getting worse—naturally, all by itself. Thus, it is the same with teams and organizations—they need constant light to grow and achieve their potential.

Without your leadership intervention in three focused areas, what is admittedly normal organized chaos in most organizations becomes increasingly unproductive. Entropy requires that leaders have to intervene—provide light, focus and accountability for execution—but in the right manner with the right tools. Without the right skills and tools, leadership is doomed to never realize the full potential of the team. This may be your single greatest calling as a leader.

The Recipe

It is my proposition that focus, execution, and your leadership make up the basic recipe for success in meeting promises to customers, shareholders, and employees. The competencies needed to be effective are:

Focus → Planning Clarity

Execution → Scoreboard & Dashboard

Me (Let Go Leadership) → Delegation, Accountability & Performance Feedback

In this chapter you will learn how the competencies of planning clarity, scoreboarding, and letting go intelligently work synergistically to achieve execution excellence. For *focus* effectiveness, master the planning clarity step after taking the required time to specify and state your strategy. *Execution* is aided by the key competency of displaying meaningful metrics all the way to front-line people. After all, it is the front line that produces the bottom line, so allow them the visual depiction of goal progress via a scoreboard. Finally, for many individuals it's all about learning how to master the key skill area of delegation—what I like to call, "letting go intelligently." Let's look at the first competency—Planning Clarity.

1. Planning Clarity

Here's a simple diagram that visually depicts why so many of us are challenged by effective planning:

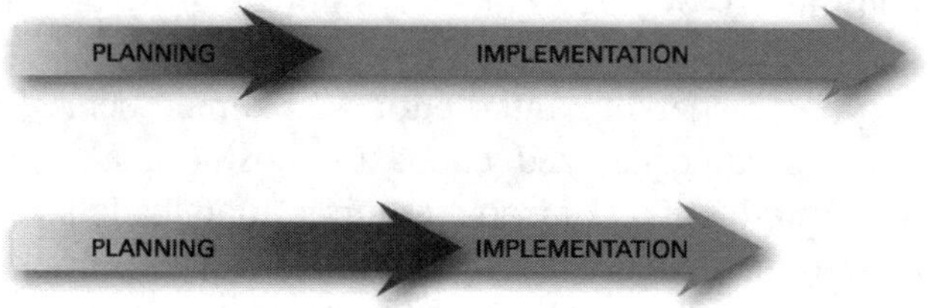

When one takes just a little more time to adequately plan, the execution of a task, a project, or an objective is reduced in the time it takes to achieve. It also reduces the *rework* along the way with fewer delays and headaches. You're shooting for effectiveness more than efficiency in proper planning clarity. Leave it to the English to say it best:

> "The nicest thing about *not* planning is that failure comes as a complete surprise rather than being preceded by a period of worry and depression."
>
> – *Sir John Harvey-Jones*

The opportunity in planning clarity is similar to having a map when setting out upon a journey. When people say to me, "Why bother planning? It'll change tomorrow..," my reply is, "When the seas are the roughest is when your navigation should be the surest." If you're facing more change today, this means your planning clarity must be sharper, more focused, and include contingencies.

2. Scoreboard & Dashboard – Performance Feedback

Can you imagine having to drive across the continent with black tape across your automobile's dashboard? You have no idea how fast you're traveling, how much gas you have—no feedback whatsoever.

Yet that is how many organizations operate today. Let's begin with two fundamental questions:

- If we asked ten people in your organization what are the top three organizational objectives or goals, would we get the same answer?
- What visible, public scoreboard (or dashboard) do you utilize to provide your people (and yourself) feedback about how we're doing?

In 2004, Harris Polling surveyed over 12,000 people in eight industries on these two questions and found these astonishing answers:

- Only 15% of those surveyed knew their organization's top goals and priorities.
- Only 16% of those surveyed said their organization provided a compelling scoreboard that depicted progress against their goals or organizational objectives.

What is your experience with how proficient most managers and executives are in performance coaching and feedback?

You may agree that this area is not the strength of most executives or managers. An interesting statistic: out of over 1.2 million people that Franklin Covey Co. has profiled (360 degree feedback containing peer, boss and subordinate ratings), the category that scored last out of seventy-seven competencies measured was "My boss provides me feedback on my performance"—dead last.

The opportunity in improved performance feedback is retaining key talent and having people who respect you and want to be mentored by you. The challenge is one of either no courage (fear is a large issue because it's not comfortable to confront poor performance) or no behavioral impact in improving performance via expert coaching.

3. Letting Go Intelligently – Delegation

It's a well-documented fact that delegation is not a strength of most managers. Michael Gerber, in his book *The Entrepreneurial Myth*, says most managers, owners, and executives are so busy working "in" the business that they fail to work "on" the business.

You cannot work *on* the business when you are constantly *in* the business reacting to both urgent and important demands and fires to put out, to-do lists that are too long, lack of clarity of goals, and leaders rarely focused on developing people because they can't let go intelligently. One rarely is promoted by mysteriously being somehow plucked up, but rather by rising on the achievements of their people like boats rising on the incoming tide.

The opportunity wrapped in improved delegation is a return of additional time to work *on* the business—time that can be spent on item# 1: planning clarity. It may take a few weeks' time, but it will happen. Delegation is wrought with real risks. The dual benefits of increased personal time on your part and building and developing your key talent outweigh the associated risks, do they not? It takes real courage to let go—more on this later.

Where's the Beef? The How-to's of Planning Clarity

Remember this line from the '70's Wendy's hamburger TV commercials? Here's the beef about planning with greater clarity.

1. **Vision** – With a blank canvass, paint a detailed, colorful picture of what your world looks like in six key areas: financial, faith, relationships, health, career, personal growth, and leisure. For an organization, it's a paragraph or two outlining your vision for the future. This step carries the rest of the plan in providing a compelling vision that makes people want to do the hard work to obtain it.

2. **Humbling look at reality** – No system can see itself in the mirror. Assess and benchmark your strengths, weaknesses, opportunities and threats. Consider one of the several superb organizational assessments in the marketplace like Gallup's Q12 or Franklin Covey's xQ (Execution Quotient) to create the impetus required to drive effective change strategies. The most important outcome of an organizational assessment is the humbling nature of the data, which tends to create the necessary *dissatisfaction* with the status quo. Effective leaders realize that only when the *PAIN* of the status quo *EXCEEDS* the pain of the change, will organizations truly change for the better.

3. **What are your PIGs – Pretty Important Goals?** What appears to be a goal is mostly something else—a strategy, loosely worded targeted direction, a recipe, tactic or project option—but not a goal. How many goals is the ideal focus? No more than three to

four PIGs is ideal. Research shows that as the number of goals exceeds three, the degree by which they are accomplished with a sense of excellence dramatically decreases.

4. **What's the plan, Sam?** Tactics, methods, and project and process management tools have been with us for decades. This is the hardest of the five steps because in essence it's the plan to implement the plan. Detailing via a timeline what deliverables are due at regularly checked (weekly) benchmarks is critical. Note that it is an iterative process, but the plan will constantly change and adapt, like a boat's sails to the winds. Then scorecard the progress—call it a "gauge" of leading indicators, not lagging indicators like financials buried in an Excel document. Leading indicators are predictors of future performance.

5. **Budget management and resource allocation** – What's the most common attribute of any great artist, athlete, or executive? Think about a perfect golf swing or tennis racket swing: it's all about follow through. Talk about budgets and money and revisit often. While that sounds ridiculously simple, I'm amazed how often meetings don't fully cover financial factors. There should be a constant dialogue on resource allocation, built upon bridges of collaboration, coordination and communication. Ask what's the best use of our limited resources today? The negotiation process is painful, but the goal is to increase the frequency of the re-evaluation—to a weekly or monthly basis.

Tracking Via Scoreboards and Performance Feedback

The opportunity in scoreboards is simple: to motivate the players to win—often without you or with less time required of you because people are self-correcting and self-accountable. Think about it. If you do not have to intervene as often or as much with your team, is that a bad thing?

To implement the use of scoreboards, begin with one goal and brainstorm a list of *leading indicators*. Leading indicators are those that are predictive of future results. Note that you may be looking at inputs (tasks, activities), but the best indicators are outputs (interim results that lead to the ultimate objective).

Next, set three targets for your scoreboard:

1. Current results and metrics
2. Target result or metric (must be quantifiable)
3. By when?

When setting up your target, it is best to set three numbers, not just one number. Why? When you set a single achievement point, you either win or lose—there is no range to shoot for. Instead, set three numbers: the minimum goal (the fence that *has* to be jumped over), the expected goal, and the stretch goal. This way, people and teams are shooting for a range that gives them more confidence and assurance. Next, set up a scoreboard with three simple colors: green for within the range of accomplishment, yellow for close but out of range given the time period, and red for being behind where one needs to be, given the deadline. When this tool is available all the way to the front-line worker, you'll find an atmosphere of self-management conducive to accomplishing objectives.

For example, if the service quality satisfaction current result is 86 on a scale of 1-100, the minimum increase would be 88, the real goal is 90, and the stretch goal would be 94. Scores below 88 would register on the gauge in red. Scores from 88 to 89 would be yellow. Scores at 90 or above would be green.

Let's say your team is in the yellow or red. It's time for some performance feedback and coaching. While this topic is much more than can be covered here, let's look at some key ingredients of effective feedback as guideposts for your team:

1. The challenge with performance feedback is that it occurs far too infrequently. Ask anyone how much guidance and counsel their manager provides—like on the days when you have *four* urgent and important priorities—and the vast majority of people say "not enough." Leaders make it a weekly habit to have brief engagement meetings to learn of progress on their goals, and to get help in prioritizing the two to three things that their employees *must* get done next week. Finally, brainstorm about new and better ways to tackle the goal and objective. Meet weekly for 10-15 minutes with your people individually. This way, a performance review becomes a summation of weekly coaching sessions instead of a revelation that this is how you feel about their performance.

2. Since leaders are responsible for everything their people do or fail to do, when your people fail, you fail. When performance slips, is it because they don't know how to or that they don't want to? One is a training issue; the other is a motivational issue. Thus, rather than talk *at* people, talk *with* them by engaging in open-ended questions to get at a root cause of the performance breakdown.

3. Never end a meeting without agreeing what your employee is going to start doing, stop doing, or do differently. Set a time to meet to review progress. Knowing that specific actions or behaviors are going to be reviewed soon at a future meeting gives the employee a sense of accountability and expectation.

4. How would you rate accountability in your organization? Measured on a scale of one to ten, I often hear an average of five, because it's dependent on the manager doing the coaching with her/his team. Accountability is not a strength of most organizations. The opposite of love is not hate, folks—it's indifference, apathy, and neglect. Discipline yourself to meet briefly each and every week, and follow up (as described earlier) for ten minutes on the three things you and your people must accomplish next week. This is best performed individually via face-to-face, phone, or virtual meeting technologies. Don't neglect people week in and week out by failing to talk. Communication is like light in a room for employees, in that they see where they are, where they need to be, and they feel *in* on things.

Letting Go Intelligently – Mastering Delegation & Achieving Empowerment

Execution is heavily affected by your ability to delegate and empower. Let's look at our personal lives first for an example. Think about what's involved when you give your car keys to your teenager the first time:

- You have confidence that they're not going to wreck the car based on previous one-on-one training. Yes, there's a front-end investment of time.
- Your teenager has an understanding of the rules, limitations, and boundaries involved, and knows there are repercussions or consequences if those rules are broken.

- You created an atmosphere where "failure isn't fatal" so that your teenager is encouraged to learn from his mistakes. Otherwise, he won't risk coming to you.

Here are the principles of delegation:

1. The receiver must see it as a forward step
2. You must be willing to let go and take a little time up front to train/work with employees
3. You must know the results expected and be able to articulate that outcome in writing
4. You must know the skills and abilities of your people
5. Sufficient authority must be given
6. Rules must be clear
7. The receiver knows that help is available
8. "Organize, deputize, and supervise" —INSPECT what you EXPECT!
9. Be sure to delegate and not "dump." A good test of dumping vs. delegating is 1) I like to do the task; 2) I'm good at it; and 3) it is important and it takes a good chunk of my time. Develop a list of tasks that meet those criteria and let go of those first.

Here are the steps to delegation and "Letting Go Intelligently":

1. Select the person—seriously consider growth involved (if high-potential employee, you'd want to delegate to him/her before you'd delegate to a person with little potential to be promoted)
2. Plan the delegation *before* you see the person
3. In meetings, delegate by these principles: results, rules, and performance standards
4. Ask for a plan of action in writing
5. Review the plan with the person and gain agreement
6. Implement the plan with your total support
7. Maintain positive follow up to insure results are accomplished

When you follow the principles and steps above, you will be more successful in delegating.

Putting the Recipe Into Action

Perhaps at several points in this chapter you said to yourself: "I know that." Understand that to *know* something and to *do* it effectively are two completely different things. Indeed, the areas of planning clarity, scoreboarding, and delegation are *not* strengths of most executives. Apply yourself to master these three key performance areas following these principles and suggestions, and your productivity and sense of accomplishment will soar. You'll *focus*, *execute*, and *lead* with the best.

Final thought: Let us all learn to let go more and ask more questions. Jacques Tocqueville said it best: "There go my people. I must find out where they are going so that I can lead them there."

When you practice humility and servant leadership you will not only find out where your people are going, but also occasionally will have the privilege of leading them there.

CHAPTER FIFTEEN

Stamp of Approval

Perception of others determines leadership success

Glenn Daughtridge

Glenn Daughtridge is the founder of Humor With A Purpose, Inc. He is a professional speaker with over thirty years of leadership experience who understands the challenges facing today's business community. In addition to humorous motivational keynote presentations, Glenn works with businesses throughout the country to develop associates' leadership, communication, and customer service skills. Glenn practices the concepts he presents as evidenced by his being honored in his community as the "Boss of the Year." He is a co-author of the book *Sales and Marketing: Proven Techniques for the 21st Century.*

Glenn believes that when people laugh, their minds are clearer and better conditioned for learning. That is why he uses humor liberally in all his presentations to make the subject of emphasis easier to remember. He also uses a blend of his country heritage and business experience to keep audiences tuned to his presentations.

Glenn's most requested keynotes are "Filling the Gap" and "F.A.C.E.S. of Success." His seminars include *Secrets of Leadership; Success Through Service; Listening, the Key to Effective Communications; Stress/Humor in the Workplace; and Effective Management Skills for the 21st Century.*

U. Glenn Daughtridge
Tarboro, NC • 252-823-8067 • www.humorwithapurpose.com

Glenn Daughtridge

Stamp of Approval

Perception of others determines leadership success

What is the perception that others have of your leadership ability? Most of us think highly of our abilities and ourselves. The key to leading a group, obtaining exceptional results, or even receiving a promotion is not based on what we think of ourselves, but on others' perception of our leadership abilities.

What is your perception of a good leader? Better still, ask those around you about their perception of a good leader. Good leaders possess attributes of integrity, fairness, sincerity, commitment, loyalty, and a willingness to listen. Great leaders are visionaries. They are confident without being arrogant. They excite and motivate associates. These leaders create an atmosphere and an attitude that produce a willing followership among others.

Are you at the top of the leadership game? Are you willing to grow and lead your associates to a higher level of productivity? If the answer is "yes," then you need to analyze why you answered yes. Is it because yes is the politically correct, expected answer, or are you truly willing to improve your leadership skills?

Leadership is often defined as the ability to guide or direct an activity. That may be technically correct, but true leadership is much more than just directing an activity. This chapter will help you analyze your own style of leadership. It will also help you develop the key characteristics of vision, listening, feedback, inspiration, loyalty, hiring, and developing a followership.

Styles of Leadership

The two basic styles of leadership are democratic leadership and autocratic leadership.

Democratic leadership characteristics include:

- respects others
- shares the reasons for instructions
- recognizes people have needs
- is tolerant of others
- inspires associates to do a good job
- shares information

Democratic leadership is positive leadership that encourages associates to be more accepting of other team members. It increases self-reliance and promotes teamwork. This type of leadership builds trust and encourages employee buy-in to new processes and projects.

Autocratic leadership characteristics include:

- believes the behavior equals the individual
- motivates with fear
- belittles others to increase power
- believes associates are lazy, doing as little as possible
- believes kindness is a sign of weakness
- refuses to share information to increase personal power

All of these autocratic leadership characteristics are negative and can result in high employee turnover, diminished production, lack of loyalty, and reduced creativity within the work group.

The leader who exercises democratic leadership skills will have the stronger, more productive work group. Obviously there are times when a good leader may need to exercise autocratic characteristics—for example, when an associate is continually late for work or is sharing confidential information with outside sources. Exercising an autocratic style may obtain short-term results and win the battle, but this approach will not win the war and will be detrimental to the long-term life of the business. Very seldom should the autocratic type of leadership be implemented. Leaders should use democratic leadership characteristics at least ninety-five percent of the time if they want to inspire loyalty and increase the self-reliance of their associates.

Leaders are self-made, not born

When Harry S. Truman became the thirty-third president, he was the first president in fifty years without a college education. His language was that of a dirt farmer and a World War I artilleryman. His background and physical appearance were unpromising. He looked more like a farmer, a bank clerk, or a haberdasher—all of which he had been. When he and a friend opened a men's clothing store, they had to close due to financial reverses. Truman refused to declare bankruptcy and it took him more than fifteen years to pay off his debts.

In 1922, he decided to improve himself by attending classes at the Kansas City Law School, but he did not obtain a law degree. He won his first local election for public office, but lost his next election. He did not give up, and in 1926 was elected presiding judge in Jackson County. Eight years later he was elected to the Senate. He went from humble beginnings to a position of great leadership. Why? Because of the perception that others had of Harry Truman. They saw him not only as a skillful campaigner, but as a person of honesty, integrity, and commitment to do what he believed was the right thing.

How can you become a superior leader? Practice the traits exhibited by Truman. He modeled hard work, self-discipline, honesty, self-improvement, diligence, and integrity. No matter the assignment, you must be willing to work hard and offer your best effort. Truman was not always successful, but his failure was never due to lack of effort.

Good leadership also requires honesty and integrity. You can learn from an early business experience of this president. When a business reversal occurred, he did not abandon his creditors. He turned a negative into a positive and so can you. When he paid off his creditors, even though it took years, Truman demonstrated integrity and gained the respect of others. They perceived that he could be trusted to do the right thing. You must be willing to do the right thing even when it becomes personally painful.

In today's changing business environment it is vital that leaders continue self-development. Do not wait for someone else to provide for your self-development. Enrolling in a class, going to a seminar, and keeping abreast of industry trends are things you can do that will improve your future as a potential leader. Harry Truman felt that enrolling in law classes would be beneficial to his public service career. Truman did not dodge responsibility and was noted for saying, "The buck stops here." As a leader, you must delegate responsibility at times. Even when you delegate responsibility, it does not give you the right to blame others when things go wrong. You are responsible for the actions of your team. The buck still stops with you.

You can become an outstanding leader by modeling the traits of hard work, self-discipline, honesty, self-improvement, diligence, and integrity. Leaders are self-made not born. President Harry S. Truman was an excellent example that effective leaders are self-made.

Vision

Great leaders know that their personal vision is not the ultimate vision of their organization. Without a vision, an organization severely limits its future potential. Simply stated, a vision is the ability to imagine and prepare for the future. Leaders should continue to share their vision with others and not worry whether the vision can or cannot happen. Many have killed their vision by not allowing others to share in the visionary process. Encourage your subordinates to be visionaries and to be more self-reliant. Leaders recognize the individuality of each associate. They mold that individuality into a proficient team striving to achieve the vision of the group. The outstanding leader can be confident that the collective vision of the team will always be greater than the leader's original vision.

Listening and Feedback

When a leader takes the time to listen to an associate, the associate feels valued as a team member. Everyone likes to think that his or her verbalized thoughts are important and worthwhile. Listening is not just hearing but an active mental process that attempts to understand the comments of another person. Studies indicate that the most successful executives are good listeners. Providing feedback is another important aspect of leadership, whether positive or constructive, because the associate feels he is being developed for future success. Feedback is a report card for the employee. It includes what is going well and what needs improvement. It is an opportunity to discuss organizational goals and how the employee's contribution will assist in obtaining those goals. Feedback should include specific suggestions for associate development.

Billy is an example of an outstanding leader with excellent listening skills. He is respected for his decisions and his intelligence. Others admire him for his integrity, fairness, sincerity, commitment, and loyalty, not only to the company, but also to his subordinates. Billy always makes an associate feel that an idea, a suggestion, or even a gripe is important. When an associate visits in his office, Billy gives that individual his total attention. He puts his work aside, holds his telephone calls to minimize interruptions, and focuses on the visitor. He provides verbal and nonverbal feedback. He does not glance at the computer to see who is emailing. One knows Billy is not only listening, but also following the thought progression of the conversation. He does not allow his associate to ramble, but moves the conversation forward because he values the time of the associate as well as his own.

Even if the thoughts shared are not compatible with the goals of the department, Billy will help you understand the reasons why an idea may not be incorporated into the department efforts. The associate does not feel stonewalled when his suggestions are not accepted. What is the associate's perception of this visit? He had an audience with his leader. His leader listened to his suggestions and gave him feedback. Billy never belittles a subordinate when he provides feedback. He shares ways the employee can contribute to departmental goals and specific ideas for personal growth. People love working for this leader and they are committed to a high performance level as a part of the team. That is a win-win situation for the leader and his subordinates.

Inspiration

A good leader inspires others. An inspirational leader causes others to see things in a new light and motivates them to outdo themselves by bringing out their best. Inspirational leaders find ways to make a mundane assignment into something more exciting. They use creativity to make work interesting and fun.

Vernon became the general manager of a department store during an economic downturn. The only thing lower than employee morale was sales results. It was the same with every store in town. Everyone talked about the poor economic conditions in the area. Business was slow everywhere. Vernon decided to change things. First, he put on a big smile for both his employees and the customers. Second, he asked his employees to put a smile on their faces. Then he instructed his employees to advise anyone who asked, "How is business?" to respond by saying, "Business is good, how may I help you?" When a customer wanted to see a shirt, the employee also showed the customer a tie and pants to complement the shirt.

Vernon began a program to reward smiling employees. Employees also received recognition for merchandise sales. All of the rewards were inexpensive fun items. Vernon set the example. He did not talk about a slow economy inside or outside the store and he always had a smile. Store morale began to change. By the end of the year this was the only area store to show an increase in sales. Vernon inspired his employees to positive results. You can motivate employees to excel by finding ways to make work fun, interesting, and rewarding. When you establish an employee procedure, model that procedure for it to be successful.

Loyalty

All companies and leaders desire loyal followers. A company needs loyalty from its work force to excel in today's business world. Leaders need dependability from associates to succeed. A good leader inspires loyalty by giving loyalty. Connie is a good leader. Subordinates know they can depend upon her to obtain necessary resources to accomplish a task. This leader enables qualified personnel to seek promotions. When errors occur, she takes the blame for departmental blunders. She does not point fingers, but guides associates in improving the process to ensure the mistake is not repeated. When the department is successful, subordinates also receive the credit. The perception of subordinates is that they are being supported and encouraged. The department works as a team to ensure success for everyone.

The best and safest way to climb the corporate ladder is not by someone pulling you up, but by subordinates pushing. They provide a solid, loyal foundation ready to support a leader and not let him fall or fail. Depending on someone above to pull you up each rung of the ladder of success results in loss of support when that person departs. When the person doing the pulling transfers out or decides to withdraw their support, you may begin to free fall and crash. If there is support from current and previous subordinates, you have a solid foundation. That foundation's perception of your good leadership will lessen the probability of a fall and increase the probability of success for all.

Secret of Success

Can you build a successful team if given the opportunity? Where would you start? What is the secret of success for a leader? Let me share my secret to leadership success: "Hire the attitude, train the skill." Individuals with a positive, can-do, willing attitude can accomplish extraordinary results. A skilled individual with a negative attitude may accomplish short-term results, but will soon sour the entire team. One negative attitude will be as destructive in the workplace as a rotten apple in a bushel.

It is very difficult to change someone's attitude. It takes a traumatic or a dramatic event to change a negative or disruptive attitude. Many individuals do work at improving or controlling their negative attitudes. Truly changing one's attitude, so that it is a part of the conscious as well as subconscious, is hard. Technology and change require workers to learn new processes. Thousands of workers successfully train to perform new skills every day. Every organization has its own culture and its own process for doing things. Successful companies continue to train and to develop their employee body.

Employees with positive, willing, can-do attitudes tend to rate their supervisors as being good leaders and their companies as good places to work. Attitude is an important ingredient for success in a changing environment. Hiring the attitude and training the skill is a perception that is truly a fact.

Developing Followership

Too often when a person becomes a project manager, that individual thinks he is automatically a leader. That is not necessarily so. A true leader must earn respect. There are some positions and titles that innately carry with them a degree of respect—for example, police officers, schoolteachers, parents, supervisors, managers, and presidents. There are people with expert knowledge who command respect and may be leaders based on their special expertise. It is important that a new manager take charge and exhibit leadership traits, otherwise an alternate leader will emerge from the members of the work group. A leader has to have followers. If a leader emerges in a work group who is different from the named leader, then that individual becomes the real leader of the group. When this occurs, the original project purpose may no longer be the objective.

Leaders develop people and are visionaries for the future. Managers manage things and results for the short term. Too often, managers and bosses believe that things have to be their way because they are in charge. They believe that subordinates have to adjust to their leadership style. Outstanding leaders recognize that this approach will not produce increased results and growth. Good leaders analyze their work group based on experience, ability, and motivation. They adjust their leadership style to meet the needs of the group. Outstanding leaders strengthen their work group by providing opportunities for individual growth to increase self-reliance.

Leaders realize that growth opportunities translate into a more knowledgeable, motivated, and experienced work force. These opportunities increase the self-reliance level of associates and develop followership. When the leader looks out for the welfare and development of the team members, there is the perception of trust and loyalty by the associates. This produces willing followers.

Putting it all together

Perception may not be factually based, but perception is reality in the mind of an individual. In other words, no matter how good of a leader you are, if your subordinates, peers, and superiors do not think you are a capable leader, your effectiveness will be severely limited.

How can you insure that others have a positive perception of you as a leader? The best way is by practicing good leadership characteristics so they become habits, not acts. Good leaders practice democratic leadership by respecting others, sharing reasons, being tolerant, and recognizing those associates who want to succeed. An individual who wants to be perceived as a good leader seeks to improve his or her skills, remembering that leaders are made, not born. They will be individuals of vision who are willing to share their visions with others. They will demonstrate fairness, trust, integrity, loyalty, positive attitude, and tactfulness. Effective leaders do not control, but inspire and influence others. One of the most important characteristics of an outstanding leader is the ability to truly listen as opposed to just hearing.

Personal leadership assessment

How can you become a superior leader? Ask yourself these questions: What is my primary leadership style? How can I practice more democratic leadership characteristics? How can I initiate development programs to increase the self-reliance level of my associates based on their individual strengths and weaknesses? How can I become a better listener? In what areas do I need additional training to be a better leader? Where can I locate a program, a book, or a mentor that will strengthen me in these areas? Ask others what leadership skills you need to improve upon and do not be offended when they tell you.

Perception of Leadership

Perception determines how subordinates, peers, and superiors respond to your leadership. Perception of you as a leader will determine if you have the support of your work group and your chances for promotion. Therefore, perception is important and becomes the basis of most of our actions and the action of others. What is the perception that others have of your leadership ability? Develop the characteristics of a great leader and perception will become a reality.

CHAPTER SIXTEEN

Success and Happiness – Yours for the Taking...
Just stop lying to yourself!

Daniel R. Fecht, PH.D.

Daniel R. Fecht, Ph.D., is a nationally certified psychologist and counselor with more than 26 years of professional experience. He has worked in both civilian and military settings in numerous capacities. Positions he has held include staff psychologist, senior behavioral science specialist (military), noncommissioned officer in charge of a neuropsychiatric service (military), mental health supervisor, child psychology consultant, civilian project manager at a police youth unit, psychology internship supervisor, mental health consultant to Head Start centers, and consultant to the National Childcare Accreditation Project.

Dan has also been affiliated with a number of national and international organizations, providing specialized services such as critical incident stress debriefings and career transition training. He is a professional speaker and trainer and has completed the "Coaching for Excellence" program at the prestigious Kauffman Foundation. He is author of *Coaching Skills for Nurse Managers, Supervision Skills for Helping Professionals, Essential Skills for Managers and Supervisors,* and *Supervision Skills for Helping Professionals.*

For the past several years Dan has provided training and consultation services to organizations in the private sector (retail, banking, gaming, health care), public sector, and to private non-profit social welfare programs. He is currently affiliated with a large private practice in Kansas City, Missouri. Dan is a member of Mensa and has been listed in *Who's Who in America* and *Who's Who in Science and Technology.*

Dan also brings to the seminar environment a wealth of experience gleaned from a variety of "non-psychology" jobs, including work as a professional entertainer. Dr. Fecht incorporates this background with his academic and professional experience to bring you a seminar that is highly informative, entertaining and inspiring!

Daniel R. Fecht, Ph.D.
Kansas City, MO • 816 753 3333 #9 • DRFecht916@aol.com

Daniel R. Fecht, PH.D.

Success and Happiness – Yours for the Taking...

Just stop lying to yourself!

Bet you've heard this one: "If you really want to, if you try hard enough, you can do anything." Sounds good, but it isn't true. There are some things that, no matter how hard one tries, will not occur. Unassisted human flight is one example. No matter how hard you or I try—simply flapping our arms will not launch us into the air. Or consider the 70-year-old who decides to win an Olympic gold medal as a sprinter. He won't win, no matter how hard he tries, no matter how much he trains. Saying that people can do anything they want to if they try hard enough involves circular reasoning. For example: "Well he didn't win the gold medal, so he must not have tried hard enough. If he had tried hard enough, he would have won." Right now, you're probably thinking: "This is rather discouraging." Cheer up. Although people can't have or do *anything* they want, most can have or accomplish more than they ever imagined if they just stop lying to themselves.

Many people don't even attempt things that would potentially improve their lives. People do not achieve or sometimes even pursue their goals or dreams for two basic reasons: real barriers and self imposed barriers.

Real barriers are objective, actual limitations. For example, many people would like to pursue a graduate degree. Some are prevented from doing so because of external barriers. Graduate school is extremely expensive, and sometimes the money simply is not available. Or maybe they have young children for whom they are caring while also engaging in full-time employment; consequently they actually do not have the time. Although there are people who have successfully attended graduate school despite staggering debt and while doing an excellent job of caring for their children, financial limitations or child care responsibilities (or both) can be genuine obstacles (real barriers). However, many people will not even attempt to pursue a goal or a dream not because of real barriers (which might be surmountable), but because of their self-imposed barriers.

Self-imposed barriers are manufactured limitations, usually based on lies. Many people miss out on opportunities of all types because of the lies they tell themselves. They don't start out lying. They start with the truth, and without knowing it, progress to lies. For example, let's revisit our graduate school aspirant. She starts with a goal: "I'd like to pursue an MBA. There are certain courses required to complete the degree. One of these is a statistics course." (True.) "Statistics is a hard subject for me." (True for most of us.) "I might not be able to pass the required statistics course." (Potentially true.) "In the program I want to attend, if a person doesn't pass stat the first time, they get one re-take and if they don't pass on that attempt, they're out of the program!" (True.) At this point she departs from the truth and unknowingly embarks on a series of lies that progressively leads to paralysis, and resigns herself to the ruts she has dug—with lies:

> <u>Lie # 1</u>: "If I failed the stat course for the second time and couldn't continue in the program, all the time, effort, and money I'd invested up to that point would have been *completely wasted*!"

That's a lie! Our person would have learned something along the way, made some contacts or friends or learned something about herself. It would be very unlikely that she would have gained nothing from the program to that point. However, the lies don't stop there.

> <u>Lies # 2, 3, 4 & 5</u>: "If that happened, I'd be devastated. Everyone would know I'm not very bright. I'd be so embarrassed I'd never be able to hold my head up again! It would just kill me!"

The mind believes anything we tell it. Now our graduate school aspirant's life is on the line. Only a fool would enter graduate school under those circumstances. Any time we find ourselves over or under reacting it's probably not the situation, but our assessment of it (what we're telling ourselves about the situation), that leads to our inappropriate, dysfunctional, or exaggerated emotional reactions.

You may have heard of Albert Ellis. He is a psychologist who early in his career practiced a form of therapy called psychoanalysis, but he was dissatisfied with the results he was getting with his patients. He developed what he considered to be a more effective type of therapy based on one statement made by the philosopher Epictetus, who said that it is not the events in peoples' lives that cause them misery, but what they tell themselves about such events. Ellis' approach is called Rational Emotive Behavior Therapy.

In a nutshell: We can't control how other people or the world behave, but we can control our thoughts about events (or anticipated events in our case), and therefore our emotional reactions to those events.
It's a simple ABC model.

A = The Event (or anticipated event)

B = The Thoughts or attributions about the event or anticipated event

C = The person's Emotional Response

Most people think that A causes C: "Because my plan didn't work out (A), I'm devastated (C)." In actuality, people are not devastated (C) because their plans didn't work out (A). They're devastated because of what they're telling themselves (B) about the fact that the plans didn't work out. Ordinarily, if the emotional response (C) is inappropriate or out of proportion to the event (A), the thoughts about the situation (B) are irrational.

The task, then, when analyzing your self-talk, is to distinguish real barriers from self-imposed barriers. It's a three-step process, summarized as DDR:

1) Discover the irrational thoughts surrounding the event or anticipated event.

2) Dispute the irrational thoughts.

3) Replace the irrational thoughts with more realistic, rational ones.

Here's how it applies in an everyday situation: Many people, even highly intelligent, accomplished individuals, recoil at the thought of giving a speech. I understand that in some surveys people indicate that giving a speech and dying are equally appealing events. Let's see why this is so using our ABC model.

A = "I have been asked to give a speech." (the event)

B = automatic, unchallenged, irrational thoughts (here's where we implement the DDR process)

C = "I'm petrified! I can't do it! I must find a way to avoid this intimidating task!" (emotional response)

Again, many people would say that the individual is anxious, afraid, or intimidated (C) because he has been asked to give a speech (A)—not so. It's what is happening at B that is causing the emotional reaction (C). When working with clients to help them understand and remove their self-imposed obstacles to success, I say it's what is going on B'tween the ears that counts. Let's take a look at the litany of lies going on in B.

"If I got up in front of a group of strangers, I'd be nervous." (Probably true.)

Being somewhat nervous isn't all bad—it means you care. By the way, reinterpret this for yourself as excitement and it won't seem so unpleasant.

"I might, because of my nervousness, forget what I want to say." (Possibly true.)

"If I forget what I want to say, I'll make a complete fool of myself." (Could happen—although making a complete fool of oneself takes some doing.)

LIES START HERE!

"IF I MAKE A FOOL OF MYSELF, I'LL LOSE PROFESSIONAL STANDING AMONG ALL MY PEERS! I'LL BE RUINED! I'LL NEVER BE ABLE TO HOLD MY HEAD UP AGAIN! I WON'T BE ABLE TO STAND IT—IT WILL JUST KILL ME!"

Note that the individual in our example lapsed into a series of lies, which, if accepted without evaluation, will put him into a very uncomfortable, possibly almost paralytic state. Now that we have discovered the lies, let's dispute them.

Lie #1: IF I MAKE A FOOL OF MYSELF, I'LL LOSE PROFESSIONAL STANDING AMONG ALL MY PEERS. Really? Probably not. Dispute the irrational thought. His prowess as a public speaker might be questioned; his professional status among a few peers might be negatively affected, but probably not. It is highly unlikely that anyone's professional status would decline in the eyes of all peers because he made an unconvincing presentation. We replace lie #1 with something reflective of the preceding rational alternatives, such as "If I make a fool of myself, my status among some peers might be negatively affected, but certainly not among all of them."

The DDR process is then completed with the remaining lies.

Lie #2: I'LL BE RUINED! *Ruined* means to be made totally useless, no longer having utility or merit. Even if lie #1 turned out to be true, would the person be totally ruined? He might be greatly inconvenienced. There is a remote possibility that he would suffer a setback in his professional career. But ruined? Nope. The irrational thought is disputed and replaced with: "The worst thing that could happen would be a setback in my career, but I certainly would not be completely ruined."

By now, you can probably apply the DDR process to the remaining lies.

Lie #3: I'LL NEVER BE ABLE TO HOLD MY HEAD UP AGAIN! Unless the individual develops some sort of orthopedic problem from flailing around while trying to find the right words, he will probably be able to hold his head up again.

Lie #4: I WON'T BE ABLE TO STAND IT—IT WILL JUST KILL ME. The only thing anyone won't be able to stand is that one thing that *will* kill him. The discomfort a person might experience from looking foolish in front of his peers, or even losing status among her peers, while unpleasant, is very unlikely to kill him.

By the way, this chapter is based in part on my academic training, but it's written from the heart, since I've been applying the principles for many years. I'm primarily a seminar leader at this time. As far as I'm concerned, it's the best career I could have—short of becoming a matinee idol or professional athlete, both of which are unlikely. Many of my colleagues are intrigued with my career and have said something to the effect that they might give the seminar business a try some day. Very few ever will. Some will be prevented by external barriers, but I believe many others will miss out on what could be a wonderful opportunity because they fear rejection by the audience.

The ABC model can also be used to remove self-imposed barriers to success and happiness in one's personal life. For example, the fear of rejection keeps many from pursuing social opportunities. Upon seeing a desirable person of the opposite (or same?) sex, many people would say to themselves, "He/she certainly seems attractive; however I can't approach that person because I would surely be rebuffed and I couldn't stand that!"

That is one possible lie and one sure lie. Possible lie: "I would surely be rebuffed." Maybe our person would be rebuffed, but it's not certain.

Sure lie: "I couldn't stand that!" Yes, they could. They might be a bit crestfallen, even hurt a bit, but they would survive the disappointment.

On the subject of success in social situations—I have not always been the incredibly handsome, dashing Tom Cruise look-a-like pictured on the back cover (that's a joke, of course). Never been a "looker" plus I'm rather short (5'5" on a tall day). During my adolescence and early adulthood, I had very little money. Wasn't what one would consider a "catch." Had a very hard time getting dates with any girl. I'd usually start by asking girls who were rather average—who almost always said "no." After exhausting my "average" list, I'd lower my sights and expectations. One day, after getting "no" from all of the below average choices, the light bulb came on. "If I'm going to be told "no," I reasoned, I might as well go for broke."

I called cheerleaders, homecoming queens and sundry other "ultra-desirable" types, who often had a difficult time determining with whom they were conversing. Predictably, many said—you guessed it—"No!" A few even laughed at the prospect of going out with me. However, a surprising number said "why not?" and went out with me. Some turned out to be vacuous and boring. Others went out with me once and never did again. However, there were a few I dated on an ongoing basis—much to the amazement and envy of my friends. I remember being out with one 5'9" absolutely beautiful young woman. She had done some modeling, been in several pageants and so forth. I asked her what had prompted her to say "yes" when I asked her out. Her response: "Because you had the guts to ask." I wasn't particularly gutsy—I had simply come to the realization that I had nothing to lose by asking. Please forgive me for that walk down memory lane. I do believe that it helps to illustrate my point.

When you find yourself inhibited about trying something, whether it's applying for a better job, entering into a new business venture, writing the great American novel, introducing yourself to that attractive stranger, or even singing karaoke (a secret longing for many, to be sure), ask yourself if the reason you "can't" is due to real or self-imposed barriers.

Cautionary Note:

Once you master your "ABC's," you will become much freer, even more adventuresome, and willing to take reasonable risks. Let's talk for a minute about reasonable and unreasonable risks. The reasonable risks I'm talking about aren't really risks at all. They involve doing the things we fear when the fear is due to the irrational statements we're making to ourselves about possible outcomes. Unreasonable risks involve genuine, unnecessary and extreme risks to our physical, moral, spiritual, ethical, or financial well-being.

For example, there are currently a number of reality shows on television that feature contestants engaging in highly dangerous and sometimes disgusting stunts. To me, participation in one of those shows involves unreasonable risks. The contestants could be injured or killed, plus eating worms on television may seriously affect their credibility in other endeavors. Similarly, a person who's fallen behind on financial obligations and borrows several thousand more dollars, flies to Las Vegas and bets it all on a number at the roulette wheel, is foolhardy. Granted, there are entrepreneurs who take great financial risks, even risks that others would consider foolhardy. However, those risk takers have generally considered their options and are prepared to deal with undesired outcomes.

A few final thoughts about "oral hygiene." No, we are not talking about brushing and flossing; we're talking about the words we use. Be careful about using extreme words, imperatives, et cetera. Words and phrases such as must, have to, awful, terrible, and the worst thing that could happen are examples. Instead, consider alternatives such as desirable, preference, inconvenient, unpleasant, unfortunate, when describing situations and referring to outcomes or potential outcomes. Imperatives and absolutes are almost never accurate. For example, "I *must* get there by 8:00. If I don't my life will be ruined." Probably not true, but these lies will throw the individual into a state of near panic. Instead, consider: "I really want to get there by 8:00: If I don't, I may experience negative consequences."

So that's it. Whenever you find yourself hesitant or anxious about a potential professional or personal opportunity, simply apply your "ABC's." It takes some practice, but when you start using the method regularly, you will begin experiencing levels of happiness and success you never thought possible...and you won't be lying to yourself!

Here's to your ever-increasing success and happiness!

Note: Rational Emotive Behavior Therapy has many other useful applications. To learn more, pick up any of Dr. Albert Ellis' many books.

CHAPTER SEVENTEEN

Flying Past the Unknown Hurdle

Grooming your successor sets you up for promotion!

Cynthia B. Stotlar,
M.ED., SPHR
and
Kristin Scott,
M.S.M., PHR

Cynthia Stotlar is the president of Creative Business Solutions, an HR and IT consulting firm in Topeka, Kansas, and co-author of the book *Career Compass for Women*. Cynthia works as both an HR consultant and trainer for her clients. She is dedicated to improving the organizational climate and overall performance.

Kristin Scott is a human resources consultant and trainer. She brings enthusiasm and life to any project. Kristin specializes in developing client relationships for the long-term by connecting with them to understand their needs and desired outcomes. Kristin has extensive experience providing workforce solutions through staff development and training, recruitment, retention, employee relations, and team building.

Cynthia and Kristin have both served as President of the Society for Human Resources Management of Topeka and have been honored as Topeka's HR Professional of the year! They are active in SHRM National and the Topeka Chapter, plus their local Chamber of Commerce.

As business consultants, Cynthia and Kristin assist organizations to achieve stellar results through creative high value HR and IT solutions. Their chapter teaches you how to improve your own chances for promotion by readying your successor.

Creative Business Solutions
Topeka, KS • 800-635-2310 • www.CBSKS.com

Cynthia B. Stotlar, M.ED., SPHR & Kristin Scott, M.S.M., PHR

Flying Past the Unknown Hurdle

Grooming your successor sets you up for promotion!

There are many hurdles in your path to promotion. Developing the skills a new job requires, networking with the right people, being visible and developing a reputation for getting things done were all hurdles that popped to the top of our minds. But there is an often overlooked or unknown hurdle each of us faces on our race to success.

We have both witnessed this unknown hurdle preventing promotions at every level of the organization from front-line supervisor to vice-president. What is it? Not having a well-trained successor is the unknown hurdle and possibly the last hurdle you will need to clear before racing to the finish line.

You may think that by making yourself indispensable in your current position, you are setting yourself up for a promotion. But the fact is that you may be *too indispensable*. If the management selection team is sitting around the table discussing who should be promoted, you don't want them saying, "We could never do without Sheila here—she's indispensable!" You want them to say, "Bob has groomed his staff to handle things when he's gone. We could promote him and then promote someone in his area to take over! That gives us two promotional opportunities and allows us to hire someone into a lower-level spot."

Take this quiz to see where you are in terms of flying past the succession hurdle.

I can have someone trained...	**Already Done**	**Tomorrow**	**Next Month**	**Next Quarter**
1. On my main job function(s)				
2. On required reports				
3. On the key expectations of my current role				
4. On working effectively with my current manager				
5. To assume responsibility over my entire job function				
6. To effectively lead the staff				
7. To achieve the desired results				
8. To move the team forward				

Congratulations to those of you who have already groomed your successor! You are on well on your way to flying across the finish line! Now you need to let your manager know it and start asking for additional projects that will set you up for success.

Condolences to those of you who haven't. You have more work to do. When we coach managers wanting to move up, we have noticed that many of the unsuccessful ones have a certain mindset, or have made wrong assumptions that tend to trip them up at the starting gate. It is often your mental game that needs work; so the first task is to change your mindset.

Get Out of the Gate – Change your Mindset

Information is power so I should hoard it.

One assumption in need of change is that information is power and that powerful people shouldn't share. If your employees don't know what is going on, they can't help. If every call needs your intervention, if every meeting needs your personal presence, then you are too busy to focus on developing your own skill set. Not sharing information creates an uncertain and fearful work environment and contributes to turnover.

The best way to empower staff, make them feel important and a part of the team is through full, complete and honest communication. Truly powerful people use all the resources around them and that includes making the most of their staff's talents.

If I want it done right, I must do it myself.

Another wrong assumption is that mistakes can't be allowed so you must do everything yourself to ensure it is done perfectly. Those of you who make this assumption never invest time training your staff to assume more responsibility. This sets you up to be needed, but not promoted. We all learn best from mistakes, as those lessons are often painful enough to remember. Set up checks to lessen the chance something is released in error. Start using a "Lessons Learned" concept after every project so you can be better next time. The "Lessons Learned" concept allows everyone on the team to objectively discuss what went well and what could be improved. It is also a great tool to use when training new staff to avoid repeating lessons already learned.

I'll put myself out of a job.

Another assumption is that if you train a replacement, you will be superfluous and find yourself outplaced. This is one that holds many back after all the downsizing companies did in the 80's and 90's. What happens is that when you have trained others to assume more responsibility, it frees you up to volunteer to take on more yourself. You will have time to tackle those highly visible projects that can make your career. Your manager will love you for offering to assume more responsibility and the management team will take notice that you are accomplishing great things!

So how do you fly past this unknown hurdle and set yourself up for promotion? Here's the plan:

Evaluate your staff for promotion potential

1. Determine who is interested
2. Do a skill gap analysis to determine training needs
3. Jointly set a plan for staff development

Groom your staff

4. Communicate your expectations
5. Implement the development plan
6. Give feedback via "Lessons Learned"
7. Access overall progress periodically

Groom yourself

8. Set a plan for development over the next year and beyond
9. Recognize your strengths and weaknesses
10. Ask your manager what he/she wants to see from you

Now let's get down to the details of how to make this work.

Evaluate Staff Potential

Determine who is interested in being groomed.

Don't assume just because you want to get promoted that everyone on your team feels the same. Have a face-to-face and ask each team member these questions:

- What are your personal career goals?
- Where would you like to be in one year? Three years?
- Have you thought about going into management or working at a higher level?
- Can you see yourself assuming my position in the future? Why? Why not?
- Would you want to be groomed for bigger and better positions?

Do keep in mind it should be OK if the team member does not want to move up at this time.

Do a gap analysis to identify improvement opportunities.

First, determine what skills and knowledge are needed for someone to move up into your position. Then analyze the performance gaps for those who are interested in moving up. We recommend you groom more than one potential successor, as life is uncertain.

For the soft side of management, we recommend using diagnostic tools to assist. Using a 360-degree performance feedback tool is very valuable for anyone already in a supervisory role. A 360-degree evaluation gives you insight into both how the person is perceived by peers and other staff in terms of his/her ability to produce results, manage change, be an effective leader, communicate effectively, and more. The evaluation we like is CheckPoint™ by Profiles International. It analyzes the person's strengths, identifies improvement opportunities and provides prescriptive advice on how to improve. Plus, the CheckPoint system has e-learning modules that correlate to competencies measured for development purposes.

Jim Collins, in *Good to Great*, indicated that a crucial factor to success is getting the right people on the bus and the wrong people off. A study published in the *Harvard Business Review* concluded that Job Match more accurately predicts job success than any of the commonly accepted factors, such as education, experience, or job training. Matching people so they fit the work they do builds productivity and job-satisfaction and diminishes negative factors such as stress, tension, conflict, miscommunication, and costly employee turnover.

Two other tools we particularly like for staff development are personality assessments and total person potential analysis. Two we like are the Performance Indicator™ and the Profile XT™. These tools provide tremendous insight into individuals and aid in grooming staff for future responsibilities.

- The Performance Indicator measures five key personality factors and their impact on seven critically important aspects of success in business. Productivity, quality of work, initiative, teamwork, problem solving, and response to stress and conflict plus work motivation are assessed. The report helps you understand how an individual is effectively understood, motivated, and managed.
- The Profile XT is a multi-purpose total person assessment that is used for selection, coaching, training, promotion managing, and succession planning. It is a powerful and dynamic management tool that employs 21st century technology to put the right people

in the right jobs. It measures the job-related qualities that make a person productive – thinking and reasoning style, behavioral traits, and occupational interests.

Build your relay team.

Once the gaps are identified, a plan for bridging the gap can be developed. See the example below. Do remember to *jointly* develop the plan. Prescribing it lessens enthusiasm. If you jointly develop it, you are simultaneously increasing commitment and buy-in.

Example Gap Analysis and Development Plan

Needed Skill or Knowledge	Current skill level or knowledge	Gap?	Activities to Bridge the Gap
Budget forecasting	Has done work unit budget	Minor	Include in next budgeting process
Staff Schedules	Has done staff schedules when I was absent	None	None needed
Hiring Process and Interviewing Skills	Has never been involved in the hiring process	Significant	Send to HR 's overview session on the hiring process Send to interviewing skills workshop Have sit in on next series of interviews

Grooming

Communicate expectations.

Communication is essential to success here. If the employee doesn't understand why you are suddenly sending him/her to training or assigning more and more difficult tasks, you won't get the desired results. Communicate your expectations. This includes communicating that you don't expect everything to be perfect the first time and that you will be there to assist. The old throw 'em in the pool to sink or swim is not a good model.

Implement the development plan.

While outside training sessions, books etc., may help groom your successor, it is real world application projects that make the difference.

Delegation is an excellent grooming tool when used well. It is also a path to promotion for both of you. We often feel guilty when we delegate. We worry over assigning "our" work to someone else. But if you're the manager, it is your job to develop your staff. What better way to do that than delegate projects that allow them growth? If you have high control needs, you're saying, "But I can do it better and faster myself!" Well, that's usually true for the first time, but with practice, your staff will develop those same skills. Grooming is a win-win. You accomplish more, work at a higher efficiency level and ready yourself for jumping that next hurdle. Your staff develops skills they otherwise might not have the opportunity to develop. We have both been sincerely grateful to previous managers who delegated significant projects to us as learning tools.

When preparing to delegate, look for…

Developmental Tasks

Think of the skills needed for someone to move up in your organization and then look for ways to assign tasks requiring those skills to your staff. For example, if written communication skills are a must, start delegating correspondence, reports and proposals. If verbal presentation skills need work, then start delegating presentations.

Perk Tasks

Some projects can be a perk to the person assigned as they provide him/her with better visibility in the organization or allow the opportunity to stretch. Think of ways to use delegation as a reward. It definitely grooms that person.

Repetitious Tasks

Tasks that you have to do often give you a better return for your training investment time. Assign reoccurring tasks such as monthly reports, writing procedures or policies, and correspondence, etc. If you take two hours to train someone, but the task frees up three hours per month, that's a good return on your training investment.

Unpleasant (to You) Tasks

Typically, if you hate the task, you tend to put it off and never do it. Chances are these tasks aren't getting done now. You may have someone on staff that really likes that type of work and would be pleased to do it. That makes it a win-win!

Here are some tips to make delegation work for you, so your staff crosses the finish line ahead of the pack.

- **Review your "To Do" list daily.** Decide which tasks could be delegated right now without any additional training. Delegating these frees up your time to groom and mentor potential successors.
- **New skills acquired by staff.** Employees may have a passion for design, even though this is not something they have responsibility for in their present position. However, they volunteer with outside organizations developing brochures and recently learned new software techniques. If you can incorporate this into their existing job duties, you have just increased their value to the organization and their loyalty.
- **Play to staff passion.** Individuals may have the best skills and abilities at particular tasks and they are your *ideal* person to get the job done; yet if they have no passion for the assignment it will be done sloppily. Get to know your staff interests, remembering that skills can be taught, but passion cannot.
- **Determine who is best to do the task.** If you have more than one potential successor, we recommend you select the one with the highest need to develop this skill.
- **Set clear, realistic goals for completion.** Set the timetable for completion so there is enough time for proofing and rework if needed. This is not the time to dump and run. Since you are using this as a growth opportunity, build in the time to discuss the why's behind the tasks.
- **Communicate the assignment clearly.** If you have an idea of what the project is supposed to look like, share your vision. Don't expect your person to have ESP. If you have previous examples, discuss what you liked or didn't like about each one to develop guidelines for how the next should be done.
- **Allow mistakes.** If you have allowed time to proof for mistakes and for minor rework to be done, this won't be a huge issue. A killer is to take the project back and complete it yourself when it isn't perfect. Allow the person you assigned to re-do it. Remember this is all about

learning and "practice makes perfect." Plus, they will not be willing or interested in working on future assignments if you beat them up.

- **Help solve problems as they arise.** Let your staff know you are available for problem solving and encourage them to discuss problematic issues with you. Practice the phrase: "What do you think you should do to resolve that?" until you have it down pat. Don't give your own answer immediately. Ask about his/her opinion. If he/she is on track, congratulations are in order. If not, you can provide insight into how you would resolve the problem.
- **Set up "checkpoint" meetings.** Review progress and answer questions or concerns.
- **Let the employee reverse decisions.** This allows others on the project to see him/her as in charge.
- **Give the authority to carry out the assignment.** If you have a budget, share what it is. If there are certain criteria that must be met to be acceptable, share that. If certain people need to be involved to ensure success, allow contacts to be made. Nothing is more frustrating than having to constantly stop working to get permission for the next step.
- **Provide latitude for imagination and initiative.** This makes the assignment much more fun and you may be pleasantly surprised to see the results!
- **Allow the person to take credit for the assignment.** Nothing undermines the process more quickly than you taking all the credit for their work! You recognizing their abilities and talents make YOU look good, too. After all, you groomed a great successor!
- **Reward results.** Everyone likes a sincere thank you but think of even more creative ways to show your appreciation.

Do "Lessons Learned"

After each assignment, sit down and have a frank and open discussion on what went well and what could have been done better. As they say: Hindsight is always 20-20. So we should take the opportunity to clearly see the project. We use this approach in our office and find it very helpful for the next project. (See the example on the next page.) Keep in mind that you MUST document for the positives as well as improvements or it will rapidly become a demoralizing discussion rather than a motivating one.

Lessons Learned

Date
Project

Did we accomplish the goal?

Did we come in on time? ____ Under-budget?______

What went well?

What could be improved the next time?

How could we add value to the next project?

Periodically Assess Progress

While you certainly want to assess each project as it is completed, you also want to assess the overall development plan results. Set up quarterly or six-month reviews to determine overall progress. Then you can revise the plan as needed. Some successors will be jumping hurdles faster while others may need one-on-one coaching. This keeps the overall goal in mind and will help you both stay focused.

Groom Yourself

Now that you have your successors in training, work with your immediate manager to do you own personal gap analysis and develop your own plan for promotion! Recognize your strengths and weaknesses. Play to your strengths and use your staff to help offset any weaknesses. Be sure to ask your manager what he/she wants to see from you and start flying past those hurdles!

Summary

In summary, a hidden hurdle to being promoted is not having a successor. Take the time to develop your employees' skills and knowledge so they can be ready to jump their next hurdle when you get that call for a promotion. Even if you don't get promoted right away, it still makes your life easier and more satisfying. It's easier because you can take a day off or a vacation without having nightmares. It's more satisfying because watching people develop and become more confident in their skills is both rewarding and fun.

CHAPTER EIGHTEEN

Staying in the Eye of the Hurricane

Ten tips for successfully navigating change

Patricia Varley, M.H.S.A.

Patricia Varley is a national speaker, trainer, facilitator, executive, business and personal coach who focuses on integrating professional, personal and spiritual growth. She has successfully worked for the past 15 years with leaders, entrepreneurs, companies and national organizations in "Reinventing Success from the Inside Out" by "Reclaiming the Wholeness of People." Patricia's unique approach has helped a wide range of clients across industry lines. She opens new paths to fresh ideas, clarity of thinking, accessing their full potential and ultimately enduring achievement. Her topics go to the heart of critical issues and programs can be customized to meet the objectives of her clients.

A frequent radio and television guest and host with numerous published articles, Patricia was honored by the Connecticut Business and Professional Women as a "WOMAN of ACHIEVEMENT." She holds a B.A. in Behavioral Science from Rollins College, Florida, and a master's degree in Organization & Management and Human Services Administration from Antioch, New England.

Her areas of expertise include Successfully Navigating Through Change & Transition, Leadership Mastery, Marketing, Sales and Networking, and Work/Life Balance. Her strong leadership, coaching and communication skills in combination with her entrepreneurial spirit helped her develop an international sales and network marketing organization of 1000 distributors.

To learn more about how to stay centered and thrive in times of change and transition, please read on…

Patricia Varley, M.H.S.A.
Naples, FL • 1-800-529-0063 • www.patriciavarley.com

Patricia Varley, M.H.S.A.

Staying in the Eye of the Hurricane

Ten tips for successfully navigating change

Imagine a raging hurricane wreaking havoc and devastation all around it. Now imagine the calm eye in the center of the storm. Storm chasers and pilots report how incredibly serene it is inside that eye. Yet that is where the power is. The entire storm organizes itself around that quiet center, which drives massive change for miles in every direction.

You have just pictured leadership in the midst of change. It is serenity, focus, clarity, organization, and stability—all in the context of tremendous upheaval, noise, and fury. Do you want to be the driver in the center—or do you want to be the victim of all that chaos? The choice is entirely yours. It all depends on how far you are willing to assume your organizing power as a leader.

Even under relatively quiet circumstances, change is inevitable. But today, especially after 9/11, we live in a perpetual hurricane season, a time of incredible upheaval and challenge to the status quo. In these times of stress and uncertainty, your ability to stay focused, goal-oriented, and on purpose is stretched and challenged beyond anything you have imagined. Global, national, and local economies are shifting. Companies are expanding and contracting all at the same time. There's no such thing as job security anymore. In fact, your company's jobs could easily be shipped abroad. Senior leadership changes players at unprecedented rates. And company missions and internal corporate cultures morph at the drop of a hat.

And that's the good news. This is a fantastic opportunity for you to demonstrate your leadership. Great leadership doesn't emerge in times of peace and quiet. It shines when everyone else is on the verge of panic and despair. Great moments in history happen during these turning points, not in times of calm. Change is going to happen. Now is your chance to show the power of your vision and leadership ability—provided, of course, you stay calm and focused. Like the eye of a hurricane.

What's at Stake

These are hair-trigger times when much is at stake. Leaders often talk about significance and legacy. Times of change enable you to establish your own legacy by helping your company and your employees create the future of their dreams. The security and happiness of families depend on the wise stewardship of your company's leaders. Your local economy depends to some extent on how your company thrives during times of change. All of your stakeholders (customers, vendors, neighbors, even competitors) will be affected by the results of your management.

The reputation of your company is also at stake. You would be wise to say, "Bring it on!" to the challenges change presents. Companies thrive on innovation. And innovation necessitates change. If there is no change, no transition, no attendant chaos, then your company won't be growing. How you manage this situation will determine how people talk about your company now and in the future. Do you want your company to be a source of inspiration for decades to come or a cautionary tale?

Finally, your own career is at stake. All eyes are watching you. Your direct reports take their cues from your behavior. If you are clear, consistent, honest, sharing, creative, and on purpose, they will be, too. If you are sending out signals that you're on constant simmer and about to blow in a massive panic attack, your entire organization will be a pressure cooker. If you withhold important data and insights, don't expect your subordinates to come to you with vital ideas and intelligence.

Your superiors will be assessing the way you handle each change event. The emergency that is currently on your plate may seem like the pinnacle of problems testing your leadership abilities to the max. Don't fool yourself. Once you top that pinnacle, you'll see a whole range of new problems in the distance. How you handle this one change event tells your bosses whether they can trust you with ever increasing responsibility. In other words, this is a terrific career growth opportunity. When all is said and done, will your supervisors judge you to be full of potential and future promise of leading your company and its employees to a brilliant future?

The choice is yours. Provided you stay calm. And you can stay calm by following these ten tips.

Ten Ways to Stay in the Eye

Change is going to happen, like it or not. Following these steps of mastery will determine whether the change is going to happen *to* you or *because of* you (in a good way, of course).

1. Begin with the end in mind.

In his book *7 Habits of Highly Effective People*, Stephen Covey's Habit 2 reads, "Begin with the end in mind." Truly talented leaders know that it is not enough to respond to the challenges that their current change event is presenting to them. They must create a detailed vision of the ideal future that will result from the change event. Know exactly what you're trying to accomplish by driving the change (rather than letting the change drive you), and then work backwards from that detailed vision.

Look at change as an opportunity to custom create a new future and demonstrate leadership to your superiors. Define an endgame in which the company emerges with a stronger sense of mission, and your employees are rededicated to their own life's purpose, as expressed through serving the company's refreshed values and short and long term goals and objectives. Your entire organization stands strong with an improved reputation in its immediate community and you strengthen your own reputation as a leader who stays focused on the ideal outcome, even when everything is uncertain.

When you establish your vision for that ideal outcome, announce it to your superiors as your objective. This takes an extra dose of nerve, obviously, but you must be willing to announce your objective before that objective is realized. Then your results will be as impressive as you deserve them to be.

2. Understand and capitalize on the power of change.

Believe it or not, there's an upside to the energy contained in the change process. It gives your entire team an adventure that coalesces their spirit and focus. (If you've been to Florida, for instance, you've surely seen T-shirts worn by locals that read, "I survived the Hurricane of (fill in the blank)." These T-shirts do more than just brag about the individual experience. They serve to unify the entire community that endured the whole, terrible, change event together. Just as they're made stronger by change, the cohesive fabric of your company will be strengthened by the shared experience of the crises it faces. It gives everyone a greater sense of self and an expanded understanding of their abilities. Just as the aftermath of a hurricane reveals new horizons and landscapes, organizational change opens up new possibilities that might not have been considered otherwise.

Change also reveals aspects of your business that may no longer be serving your company's long-term objectives. The fresh wind that blows through your workplace may reveal policies, markets, and objectives that are weighing you down. Former General Electric CEO Jack Welch advises leaders to routinely cut out the bottom 10% of their business. Just as you must hack off dead limbs after a hurricane, a good blow through the company will help you spot the dead branches that clutter your business-scape and block out the sun, restricting new growth.

3. Clarify and communicate new goals and intentions.

Now that you know what the new endgame is, it's time to recruit your team to help you realize your new goals. They need to be invested in the goals as much as you are. And you need their passion and energies like never before. You may be met with resistance at first, as many employees may be trying to revert back to the old ways. But it won't be long before everyone recognizes that the future is the only path forward.

To build support for your goals, communicate them effectively to your employees. Effective communication requires two essential ingredients: repetition and inclusion. Take every opportunity to repeat, and repeat again, your core messages. Turn them into slogans. Write articles about them for both internal and external publication. Build speeches around the essential themes. Have parties to celebrate the milestones.

Don't be surprised to discover the most resistance from the company's top leadership. The changes you're proposing may represent an obliteration of the objectives they've spent the last several years—even decades—building. As frustrating as their resistance may be to you, have the understanding, and patience necessary to show them how these new evolutions will, in fact, help them achieve their goal of a prospering company. The details you're proposing to change are just that—details. The original passionate vision remains untouched.

Include everyone above you and below you on the organization chart in the development of your vision. The key is to create a sense of ownership in the outcome of this change event. The best way to promote a sense of ownership is to bring everyone into the experience of building the vision to begin with.

4. Be the change you want to see in the world.

Mahatma Gandhi was the first to utter this advice to the modern world. Now millions of people around the world embrace it as their own personal motto. It will work for you, too. People are only going to follow you to the extent that you embody and demonstrate the behaviors associated with the change you want to create in your organization. Do you want your company to stand for excellence and high-quality products for your customers? Then you must be excellent in everything you do and provide high-quality leadership both internally and externally.

Do you want a calm, resourceful team that is solution-oriented? Then you must be calm, resourceful and solution-oriented in the way you treat your employees. Do you want to break down organizational barriers and encourage everyone to pitch in where help and energy are needed, regardless of job description or leadership levels? Then you must be willing to roll up your sleeves. Be the change and others will follow.

5. Be your own learning organization.

One of my clients, the owner of a major car dealership, wanted to lead his employees with a more elevated sense of purpose and wisdom. I recommended that he read *The Four Agreements*, by Don Miguel Ruiz. He liked it so much that he bought a copy for his entire staff—over 200 employees.

Now is the time to get wise. And there's no better way to get that wisdom than through the words of thought leaders and philosophical masters. You don't have to be a professor or a high-IQ genius to guide the development of your employees. Establish the fundamental principle that ongoing learning is an essential part of this change process you're in. Bring in speakers and reading material that will help your employees imagine a better, more rewarding experience for themselves.

Start a library in your break room, filling it with books that you admire and recommended books from people you look up to. Ask your leadership to create a budget for a collection of new books and find ways to encourage all your employees to invest their personal time in absorbing the wisdom contained in those books.

6. Measure the effects of change against future ideals.

The quickest way to gain support and traction around your change initiative is to find a way to somehow quantify its value. Leaders like numbers, and if you can translate your dreams into numbers, you can go straight to their imagination with data that will truly move them. If you can assign a numeric value to the change process itself, you will then be able to tell your story in graphs, matrices, quadrants and percentages—all formats that can help you speak more effectively to superiors and other stakeholders.

Translating this adventure into the concrete successes achieved by yourself and your team will bring it full circle. Celebrating human achievements along with solid bottom-line successes creates a sturdy foundation during times of change *and* stability while expanding into future ideals.

7. Prioritize the objectives you want to pursue.

In a hurricane there are a tremendous number of things flying through the air: convertibles, wedding albums, aluminum siding, gas station signs, sail boats, weather reporters. In the confusion of this mélange of artifacts of life as you knew it before the storm, it is tempting to try to salvage anything you can. But without a plan of priorities, you could very easily grab for the wrong things. Ask yourself, what are the essential pieces on which you really need to focus? What can you afford to let go, either forever or simply for now?

Prioritizing is especially important when things are chaotic and in a state of change. It's a way for you to stay focused on what's essential for your ultimate outcome. And, from a leader's perspective, it's a valuable way to help your team stay focused on what's important as well. An essential part of prioritizing for your team is organization. Write down things, delineate processes, procedures and performance expectations for your team. Assume nothing. Omit nothing.

8. Share the burden.

It doesn't matter how long you've been established as a leader. It still takes confidence to ask for help. In fact, current economic conditions that force you to do more with less actually reward you for taking on more direct responsibility. This is not self-sufficiency. This is career suicide.

Trust your team to help move your organization through this change adventure, and be committed to empowering them. Their growth is as much an essential result of the change experience as the company's long-term viability. Again, I recognize that this is easier said than done, because when things are so uncertain you may be tempted to clamp down and seize control even more. The mark of a true leader is that you will resist the temptation to over-control.

While you're at it, throw some of the burden up the ladder in the direction of your supervisors. This might also be difficult for you to do, because it's natural to be reluctant to reveal that you need extra help. Word your request in this spirit of, "I really value your opinion and expertise, and I could use your help on this one piece of the challenge." Your leaders would be unwise to refuse.

9. Make your workplace a communication-friendly environment.

At *Fortune* magazine's Leadership in Turbulent Times conference in 2001, Harvard Business School professor Rosabeth Moss Kanter said, "Everything in process looks like it's failing." What she meant by this is that we must all have some capacity for self-doubt and compassion for each other during a time of flux. To achieve this kind of humane culture, it's essential that you make it *safe* for people to share their feelings, concerns and ideas—even if those ideas are astoundingly off the mark.

Build a workplace where everyone can talk freely and is able to both offer and receive constructive criticism. Hold weekly meetings where open communication is encouraged and valued as well as implemented into the workplace when relevant. Isolation kills dreams; but dreams thrive in an environment where everyone feels safe to share what's on their mind.

If unstructured sharing becomes too time-consuming and anxiety-producing for you or your leadership, plan regular all-hands meetings (weekly or monthly) in which free, but mutually respectful, expression is encouraged, safe, sacrosanct and confidential.

10. Practice extreme self-care.

In a time when chaos is all around you, it may seem ultimately self-indulgent to take the time to make sure you are healthy, calm, and centered. But it's a basic fact of nature: people can't give what they don't have. When you're burned out, you won't have much to give. And this is when people need the most from you. Additionally, when you take good care of yourself during times of change, people will take your example and do the same. In a sort of ripple effect, they'll take care of each other. Self-care isn't just taking care of yourself. As a leader in your organization, the steps you take to make sure you have everything you personally need to be at your most effective directly benefit the company.

Extreme self-care is not only a maintenance process; it's a renewing one. Your efforts to keep your body and mind in top shape will result in a healthier, ever self-renewing organization as well. And self-renewing organizations will be more effective and ahead of most challenges that come their way.

You've heard it all before, but this time it's extra important. Stay away from unhealthy, energy-draining foods. Exercise at least an hour a day. Sporadically throughout the day, take a few minutes to breathe deeply and think quietly.

Pay extra attention to your emotional and spiritual health as well. Meditate. Pray. Attend inspiring lectures or sermons. Make sure you keep company with optimistic people who thrive in the realm of possibility thinking.

Whatever you do, treat yourself with the grace and kindness you know you deserve. Remember that the external environment of change may be confusing, chaotic and painful. That doesn't have to touch your inner life. But your inner life can have tremendous influence on the people and circumstances swirling around you.

Remember...

Moments of great leadership emerge from times of noise, confusion and fear. It is not only what you do, it is *who you are* in those moments that creates great leaders. Inspiring leaders are not necessarily needed when all is calm, but are especially important in times of change. By adopting the ten tips for navigating through change, you and your organization will not only survive, but transform into your full potential. By embracing all the opportunities available to you and committing to continuous improvement and long term growth, you will truly be the eye in the center of the storm.

Additional Resources From Our Team of Co-Authors

POWER TOOLS

TOP EXECUTIVE COACHES PUT YOU ON THE FAST TRACK TO SUCCESS

Additional Resources From Ben Adkins

Monthly Productivity Tips – Free from www.TrainingSpeaking.com

Receive complimentary timely tips that help you improve personal productivity and develop professionally in the areas of communication, conflict resolution, leadership and more.

Dana Cost of Conflict Measurement Instrument

Request a free instrument to measure the cost of conflict in your organization. You may be shocked and surprised at the results.

Dana Survey of Conflict Management Strategies

Request this free instrument that identifies the blend of four conflict management strategies that are currently imbedded in the structure and culture of your organization.

Training and Development Services

In-house training classes delivered by Adkins & Associates are custom-designed and tailored to meet your specific employee development needs. Topics include core competencies in conflict resolution, interest-based negotiation, leadership development, performance coaching, teambuilding, customer service, presentation skills, and business writing. Guaranteed to get results.

Coaching Services

One-on-one management and executive coaching ensures leaders develop competencies needed to succeed. Coaching areas include effective relationship building, conflict resolution and mediation, and bullet-proof presentation skills.

Keynote and Workshops

Dynamic presentations for conferences, meetings and conventions include: Weaving Conflict Resolution into the Fabric of Your Organization; How to Be a Leader Instead of a Boss; Secure Your Own Mask Before Assisting Others; and People Aren't Difficult—Just Different.

CONTACT INFORMATION:

Adkins & Associates
817-370-8746
ben@trainingspeaking.com
www.TrainingSpeaking.com

Additional Resources From Karen L. Anderson

Workbook:

Living Letters: How to Make a GREAT Relationship

Books:

To Meet or Not to Meet
The Busy Manager's Guide to Successful Meetings
Proof Positive: How to Find Errors Before They Embarrass You
Magnetic Leadership
Life Compass for Women: The Indispensable Guidebook on Life Management for Busy Women

Adult Learning Programs:

Adult Learning Methods
Persuasive Presentations
E-mail Professionalism & Composition
Professional Writing Program
Technical Business Writing
Grant Writing Strategies
Grammar, Punctuation, Usage & Proofreading
How to Stay in Control in the Midst of Chaos
Customer Service: You ARE the Organization
Super Supervisory Skills for Non-profits
Empowerment and Forgiveness
Professional Protocol and Presence
Life's Lessons in Your Hands
(Other titles and topics upon request.)

Ask Karen about her customized, laminated "Concept Cards" and "Desk Mats."

ORDERING INFORMATION:

Anderson Catalyst Training Services
7923 Noland Road, Lenexa, KS 66215-2528
Office: 913-492-3881/1-866-240-3935
www.acts-ion.com
Email:Karen@acts-ion.com

Additional Resources From Charles A. Breeding

Whether you're bringing in a facilitator for an executive retreat or planning for a speaker for a National Sales meeting or customer event, you HAVE to hit a 'home run.'

~ Reduce your risks with a proven winner ~

Services Include:

- Executive and manager training, like *The Three Disciplines of Execution: From Strategy to Execution*
- Keynote and conference speaking, like *A Dull Guillotine is a Pain in the Neck*
- Change Management and Change Leadership consulting
- Customized learning and delivery, like *Focus & Execution Suite*
- Management retreats and meeting facilitation
- Executive coaching

Contact for more ideas about the *Big 3: Focus, Execution & Me*. Join over 600 subscribers to the FREE newsletter, *Monday AM Motivation* – a bi-weekly ezine of motivational stories, inspirational quotations, & recent articles of interest.

CONTACT INFORMATION:

Charlie Breeding
336.643.1115 or 866.476.1115
cbreeding @triad.rr.com
www.ccfs.biz (click on Professional Services)

Additional Resources From Jonathan Clark

Business Writing Solutions Video CD-ROM

Perfect for individual or organizational self-study! Eight disks of 40-50 minutes each containing the program Southwest Airlines, NASA-Kennedy Space Center, RadioShack, U.S. Postal Service and others schedule repeatedly. Featuring Jonathan Clark.

- CC-1 CD-ROM plus 25 workbooks $1,999.00
- CC-2 CD-ROM plus 15 workbooks $1,499.00
- CC-3 CD-ROM plus 5 workbooks $ 999.00
- CC-4 Individual pack: 1 book and CDs $ 399.00

Writing Tips Reminders at Your Desk

Handy laminated cards contain a writing idea on one side and a grammar tip on the other. Or put the ideas under your mouse and think "good writing" every time you scroll!

- CC-5 Writing Tips® cards (pack of eight) $ 9.95
- CC-6 Writing Tips® Mouse Pad $ 19.95
  (Call 1-877-398-5456 for quantity discounts)

Executive Letter Writing: A Report

If you're as worried about writing a good letter as most people, this exclusive report (with specific examples) will guide you to the perfect letter every time!

- CC-7 Letter Writing Report (in pdf format) $ 14.95

To Order:

- Visit www.scottsdaleseminars.com/products.htm for secure online ordering using your credit card
- Mail check (payable to Scottsdale Seminars) to Product Orders, Scottsdale Seminars, P.O. Box 268, Phoenix, AZ 85001-0268
- All prices include shipping and handling. Arizona residents add 8.1% sales tax

Outstanding Programs From Scottsdale Seminars

Conceived, created and written by Jonathan Clark, "The Nation's Business Writing Expert."

- Business Writing Solutions (2-day class)
- Business Grammar and Usage (1-day class)
- Report and Proposal Writing (2-day class)
- Writing Policies and Procedures (1-day class)
- Technical Writing Solutions (1-day class)

CONTACT INFORMATION:

Jonathan Clark, Scottsdale Seminars
P.O. Box 268
Phoenix, AZ 85001
1-877-398-5456
jclark@scottsdaleseminars.com
www.scottsdaleseminars.com

Additional Resources From Deb Clifford

INSPIRED PRODUCTS AND SERVICES
Available through www.inspiredpeople.com:

e-burst ™ subscription

Subscribe to our e-burst™ for free–and get messages from Deb bursting with insightful tips, recommendations and inspiration.

Strengths Tips

Download free tips to uncover your strengths. Manage your weaknesses to avoid failure, and spend your remaining development time polishing your strengths! Includes strengths matrix.

Inspired People Learning Fundamentals – white paper

A short, informative white paper that explains why 'workshops don't work.' Use these guidelines when discussing your program design with Inspired People, or for your own internal training design. $19 (US) plus tax.

e-coaching with Insights and Inspired People

Increase your self-awareness and build on your professional development. Find out your personality type, behavioral preferences and communication style. Receive the web version of the Insights Discovery profile (The Key to Personal Effectiveness) along with a 45-minute tele-coaching session with Deb. $99 (US) plus tax.

Inspired Journals

These journals can be used to capture a variety of jottings from your reflections to your "to do" list. Journal covers feature the whimsical art of Tracy-Lynn Chisholm. Each notebook is spiral bound with 150 lined pages. Great for inspiring gifts to colleagues and friends. $15 (US) plus tax, S&H.

Inspired Note cards

10 note cards & matching envelopes to inspire your colleagues. Use them to send notes of recognition while reinforcing the motivational motto on each card. The note cards present the whimsical designs of Tracy-Lynn Chisholm on the outside. Inside blank. $8.00 (US) plus tax, S&H.

CONTACT INFORMATION:

Inspired People
860-217-4566
deb@inspiredpeople.com
www.inspiredpeople.com

inspired people

Additional Resources From Glenn Daughtridge

Book:

Sales and Marketing: Proven Techniques for the 21st Century $18.00 plus S&H

Cassettes:

Fun with Glenn $10.00 plus S&H

Glenn Goes to Church $10.00 plus S&H

CD:

Glenn Goes to Church $12.00 plus S&H

Keynotes:

Filling the Gap
A humorous motivational presentation that demonstrates how the uniqueness of each one of us can be used to fill the gaps that occur in every organization.

F.A.C.E.S. of Success – (**F**lexibility, **A**ttitude, **C**ommitment, **E**nthusiasm, and **S**elf)
A fun, fast-paced presentation emphasizing personal and business success.

The Best Is Yet To Come
Audiences will leave feeling good about themselves and the organizations they represent.

Seminars:

Secrets of Leadership
Learn how to use the proper leadership style to increase productivity. Participants receive a monthly "Leadership Update" for six months that reinforces concepts.

Success Through Service
Discover the twelve (12) key essentials necessary to obtain and retain customers.

Listening, the Key to Communications
Communications is not what is said but what is understood. Learn Glenn's unique "bucket " approach to getting your ideas accepted by others.

CONTACT INFORMATION:

Glenn Daughtridge
252-823-8067
HWAP@prodigy.net
www.humorwithapurpose.com

Additional Resources From Daniel R. Fecht

Dr. Daniel Fecht is available as a speaker/trainer for various types of functions, from formal training sessions to serving as an after dinner speaker. Some of the topics he can present for your organization are listed below. The general topics can be tailored to meet your training needs.

TOPICS

- Stress Management
- Effective Communication
- Principles of Success
- Yes You Can!
- Assertiveness for Men and/or Women
- Minimizing Stress and Avoiding Burnout
- Basic Self-Protection (3-hour course)
- Maximizing Your Success and Happiness
- Goal Setting
- The Meaning of Discipline
- Conflict Management

Daniel is also available for voice-over/acting assignments.

The following proprietary courses are available only through the identified organizations.

Disruptive Behavior Disorders in Children and Adolescents—And Related Challenges (Full day) Live training or audiotape program. Live training qualifies for continuing education (CE) credit for many professions.

Coaching Skills for Nurse Managers (Full day) Live training or audiotape program. Live training qualifies for CE credit for many professions.

Available through:
Cross Country Education • 1-800 397 0180 • P. O. Box 305006 • Nashville, TN 37230-5006

Essential Skills for Managers and Supervisors (Full Day). Live training available for CE credit for groups (many professions).

Supervision Skills for Helping Professionals (Full Day). Live training or audiotape program. Live training available for CE credit for groups (many professions). Audiotape course qualifies for CE credit for individuals.

Assertiveness (CD – 1 hour 15 minutes) Can be used for informational or self-development purposes, or can be used by groups for CE credit.

Available through:
PESI HealthCare/PesiBusiness • 1-800 843 7763 • 200 Spring Street • Eau Claire, WI 54702

CONTACT INFORMATION:

Daniel Fecht, Ph.D.
1-816-753-3333 #9
P. O. Box 28191
Gladstone, MO 64118

Additional Resources From Bill Fotsch

The Game is not a gimmick, a philosophy or an attitude. The Great Game of Business© is a premiere management system that turns business into a game and puts all employees on the same field in order to win. No matter what "league" you are in, The Game will work for you. From small, privately held companies to multi-national corporations, the success of open-book management parishioners have proven that The Great Game works. The Great Game of Business has helped thousands of organizations improve not only their financial performance, but their corporate culture as well.

The Great Game of Business provides business literacy training, employee ownership training, a Two-Day experience workshop, and coaching services as well as other services to engage employees and foster higher levels of financial and corporate performance. Once a year The Great Game of Business hosts The National Gathering of Games, a conference focusing on the elements of Open-Book management.

The Great Game of Business has the following products and literature available:

- Financial Planning Module
- Huddling Module
- Recognition, Bonus, and Games Module
- Sales and Marketing Module
- Yo-Yo Company Workbook, A Financial Workbook

The following books have been published by Jack Stack, The Great Game of Business founder, or other Great Game practitioners and supporters:

- *The Great Game of Business*, Jack Stack (available in book or DVD form)
- *A Stake in the Outcome*, Jack Stack
- *Open Book Management*, John Case

CONTACT INFORMATION:

The Great Game of Business
3055 E Division Street
Springfield, MO 65804
(417) 831-7706
www.greatgame.com
Bill Fotsch
Head Coach
(859) 331-6925
bfotsch@ggob.com

Additional Resources From Ann E. Mah

Workshops available include:

- Don't Go Hunting Bears With a Stick
- It's Not Personal
- Oh, Behave!
- Managing the Challenge of Change
- Making Waves – Developing Your Own Personal Style
- Let's Do Lunch!
- Can You Hear Me Now?

Reprints of Ann's articles from *HersKansas* magazine teach you skills to navigate the corporate landscape. Over 20 articles available at www.annmah.com include:

- "Mentoring Teamwork" – Identifying a mentor to meet career goals
- "Work Past 'No'" – Play up your bartering strengths in negotiations
- "Let's Do Lunch" – A business dining etiquette primer
- "Can You Hear Me Now?" – Getting your message across
- "Lower Your Center of Gravity" – Maintaining balance in your life
- "When Bad Behavior Happens to Good People" – Dealing with conflict in the workplace
- "Career Connection" – Turn your boss into an ally.

Books:

Career Compass for Women: The Indispensable Guidebook for Women in the Workplace

Life Compass for Women: The Indispensable Guidebook on Life Management for Busy Women

CONTACT INFORMATION:

Ann E. Mah – Discover! Strategies
Office: (785) 266-9434
Website: www.annmah.com
Email: ann@annmah.com

Additional Resources From Susan Meyer-Miller

Videos

Step Up and Lead – Four part video series

Step Up and Lead features Susan Meyer-Miller, award-winning international speaker and trainer. Our corporate training videos focus on leadership skills, leadership image, mastering motivation, mediating employee conflicts, employee development and performance. Only $99.00 plus shipping and handling for all four videos.

Set includes:
Video 1: Establishing Yourself as a Leader (1 hr 45 min)
Video 2: Creating Synergy Through People Skills (1hr)
Video 3: The Leader as Coach: How to Bring Out the Best in Individual Team Members (1 hr 45 min)
Video 4: Solving Performance Problems (45 min)

Also available individually for $29.95 plus shipping and handling.

Books

SOS! 101 Solutions to Overcome Stress is our book filled with practical and humorous solutions for getting through stressful situations. Available for $6.95 + S&H

Speak with Power, Passion and Pizzaz – 222 Tips to Dazzle Any Audience. By Susan Meyer-Miller and Dr. Prasad Kodukula. $16.95 + S&H

Career Compass for Women – The Indispensable Guidebook for Women in the Workplace. 14 mini-workshops in a book with practical career advice. Coauthored by Susan Meyer-Miller. $14.95 + S&H

Life Compass for Women – The Indispensable Guidebook on Life Management for Busy Women. 16 mini-workshops with advice for managing life situations. Coauthored by Susan Meyer-Miller. $14.95 + S&H

ORDERING INFORMATION:

SpeakerUSA
Susan Meyer-Miller
Shawnee, KS
1-877-674-8446
(913) 248-1485
www.SpeakerUSA.com

Additional Resources From Meg Montford

Complimentary Articles Through Abilitiesenhanced.com

- "Life After Layoff: Three Keys for Speeding Up Reemployment" – Learn how the job loss experience mirrors the grieving process. (First published by www.6figurejobs.com, 2003.)
- "The Top 17 Signs You're Due for a Career Change (And What to Do About It)" – Get this eye-opening checklist with a free subscription to the AE News, a monthly ezine.
- "Boost Your Job Search Effectiveness" – Adopt these behaviors to rapidly find your next position. (First published by www.6figurejobs.com, 2003.)
- "Top Ten Smart Networking Tips" – Master these steps to master your career destiny. (First published by www.Netshare.com, 2003.)
- "What Would It Take to Achieve Career Success?" – Learn what career coaching is and how it quickly facilitates change to move you forward.

Professional Services

- Get Ahead of the Curve – Six-month individual career-coaching program to help you design and implement a lifelong career management strategy.
- Discover Your Authentic Vocation – Three-month individual career-coaching program to help you discover your passion and achieve a radical career change.
- Career Review – Try career coaching for one month to evaluate "what next?"
- Career Power Hour – Resolve a single issue fast in this 60-minute laser-coaching intensive.
- Professional Resumes and Career Portfolios created by certified and trained writers.

Seminars

- *Communication Styles: Understanding Yours and Others*
- *Prepare or Despair: Do Your Interviews Get Offers?*
- *Writing Resumes That Get Interviews*
- *Give More Than You Get: The Key to Great Networking*

ORDERING INFORMATION:

Abilities Enhanced®
Phone: 816-767-1196
Email: meg@abilitiesenhanced.com
Website: www.abilitiesenhanced.com
Blog: www.careerchaos.com
P. O. Box 11823, Kansas City, MO 64138

Additional Resources From David E. Nelson

EQ In Action Profile© – This emotional intelligence assessment tool was developed over a four-year period, using a rigorous development process, which included input from hundreds of professionals throughout North America. It is totally behavioral based and is taken on-line with a booklet sent to you. One interpretative session with David, a certified "Learning in Action" trainer is part of the $150 cost. This is an excellent resource for executive coaching. For additional information visit www.learninginaction.com.

Leadership Competencies Card Deck© – This attractive boxed card deck of 41 essential competencies includes "suggested use" cards and a quick guide overview of the competency model. Can be used as the basic criteria for hiring, performance management, position descriptions, succession planning, training objectives, promotion, personal development, etc. This can be used with a "Polaris 360 Survey" and is priced according to services desired. For more information visit http://www.orgsysint.com.

Inscape Profiles© – "Personal Profile System DiSC," "Managing Work Expectations," "Time Mastery Profile," "Dimensions of Leadership Profile," "Team Profile" and many others. David is an Inscape distributor. For more information see the link on his website.

Most requested training programs:

- Appreciative Supervision
- Living a Fully Human Life
- Emotional Intelligence
- Team Building
- Appreciative Leadership

On The Human Agenda Web page (www.humanagenda.com) you can download coaching resources, a variety of book and movie reviews, information on emotional intelligence, worksheets for appreciative inquiry, reflections on current events and a collection of photographs. This site is both a professional and personal resource.

CONTACT INFORMATION:

David E. Nelson, D.Min.
The Human Agenda
Office: (816) 453-3835
Fax: (816) 453-3936
5735 N. Clinton Lane
Kansas City, MO 64119
david@humanagenda.com
www.humanagenda.com

Additional Resources From Jim Peal

Keynotes and Workshops – that enlighten, entertain, and educate while providing people with practical tools they can use immediately.

Daring to have the Real Conversation: Beyond Driving Performance to Inspiring Performance –www.therealconversation.com

There's no Harmony without Diversity: The 3 A's of Diversity: Awareness, Attitude & Action – Key tips for appreciating and leveraging diversity in your organization

On-Target Communication: Understanding and leveraging communication styles in the workplace

Principled Negotiations and Compelling Partnerships: Skills based course that teaches you the essential verbal aikido skills to turn any situation around

Hiring the best – A leader's toughest job: Using SelecSys Software System to hire the best people into your company

Services through The Peal Consulting Group

- Qualitative 360, Leadership Development Process
- Executive Coaching
- High Impact Presentation Skills Training
- Team Based Strategic Planning Facilitation
- What's your style? – Team Based Communication Skills
- Organizational change and evolution

Products through The Peal Consulting Group

- *Daring to have the Real Conversation* – Instructional DVD, Demo DVD
- *SelecSys* – Communication Profile, Individual and Team/Group

CONTACT INFORMATION:

Jim Peal, Ph.D.
Peal Consulting Group
2202 Damuth Street Suite 3
Oakland, CA 94602
510-336-0417
james@peal.com
www.peal.com

Additional Resources From Jolene A. Savage

ETIQUETTE TRAINING

Decorum • Refinement • Distinction • Poise • Charm • Protocol

Services are offered to executive, corporate and school-age clients.

Seminars
Workshops
Classes
Etiquette CDs
Books
Gift certificates
Individual consultation

All offerings can be customized to meet the customer's requirements. For details, see www.socialgraceks.com.

Cover photograph by KELA Photography.

CONTACT INFORMATION:

Social Graces – *The Gift of a Lifetime*
Jolene A. Savage
Phone: (785) 478-3364
Fax: (785) 271-6359
email: socialgraces@sbcglobal.net
www.socialgraceks.com

Additional Resources From Valerie Simpson

SERVICES

One-on-One Training and Coaching
Efficiency Evaluations
Hands-on-organizing of any environment; auto, home, office, time...
Small Business Consulting
Job Description and Procedures Manual Writing

PRODUCTS

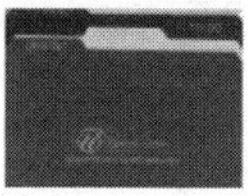

Priority Folders©

"The solution to your inbox nightmare" Prioritize your inbox documents in these six vinyl folders. The system is designed to provide you with versatility. Use them interchangeably in your office, home, auto, etc.

The Ultimate Filing System©

A computer-based filing system that will transform the paper and file-management processes you are currently using in your business. *"Find any document in your office within seconds."*

The Ultimate Residential Filing System©

A computer-based filing system that will transform the paper and file-management processes you are currently using. *"Find any document in your home within seconds."*

17 Professional Organizers Tell All © 2nd Edition

This book is a well-organized, easy to read, high-value reference tool for busy people! (2nd Edition)

We invite you to subscribe to our FREE monthly online eZine. Simply visit our website and click on "Newsletters." *All our products are available on-line. Simply visit www.Organize-U.com*

CONTACT INFORMATION:

Organize-U Consulting, Inc.
602-ORGANIZE (212-0857)
www.Organize-U.com
P.O. Box 16283
Phoenix, AZ 85011

Additional Resources From Cynthia B. Stotlar and Kristin Scott

Creative Business Solutions areas of expertise are:

Consulting

- HR Audits
- Internal Investigations
- Process and Technology Consulting and Re-engineering
- Hiring Process and Orientation Design
- Employee Engagement Surveys
- Focus Groups
- Succession Planning
- Customer Service
- Employee Recruitment and Retention Planning
- Team Function

Products

- 360 Performance Management Systems
- Honesty, reliability and work ethic assessments for pre-employment
- Work expectations tools to improve employee relations
- HRIS Software that offers Employee Self-Service, E-Recruiting and either in-house or outsourced payroll capabilities to meet your needs!

Custom Designed Training

- Leadership
- Supervisory
- Customer Service
- Team Building
- Personalities
- Diversity
- Plus, On-Line E-Learning

Creative Business Solutions' purpose is to improve the quality of your work life through creative high-value Human Resource and IT solutions. We accomplish this with a variety of tools in our power belt! We are licensed distributors for Best Software, Inscape Publishing, and Profiles International products.

CONTACT INFORMATION:

Creative Business Solutions
100 SE 9th Street Topeka, KS 66612
800-635-2310 or 785-233-7860
www.CBSKS.com
Cynthia.Stotlar@CBSKS.com
Kristin.Scott@CBSKS.com

Additional Resources From Patricia Varley

Customized programs are available on the following topics:

- One-hour keynote
- Half-day seminars and workshops
- Full-day seminars and workshops
- Group facilitation
- Business, Executive and Personal Coaching and Group Teleclasses

Seminars and Workshops:

- Successfully Navigating Through Change & Transition
- Leadership Mastery: Transforming the World at Work
- Marketing & Networking for Success: A Heart-Centered Approach
- High Energy Living: Creating a Balanced Life
- Women & Self-Leadership: Mastering Self to Empower Others
- There is Only One of You in All of Time: 10 Heart-Centered Principles for Living the Life You Desire

Complimentary articles via www.patriciavarley.com

"Successfully Navigating Through Change & Transition"

"Leadership Mastery: Transforming the World at Work"

"Marketing & Networking for Success: A Heart-Centered Approach"

"High Energy Living: Creating a Balanced Life"

CONTACT INFORMATION:

For more information on Patricia Varley and her upcoming programs, CD series, books, workbooks and fees please visit –
web: www.patriciavarley.com
email: patricia@patriciavarley.com
call: National Voice Mail 1-800-529-0063

Additional Resources From Kate Zabriskie

Signature Keynotes:

- Choices Aren't Chances – A 50 Minute Attitude Adjustment
- But My Brass Ring Was Hollow – Failing Forward for Success

Seminars and Training Programs:

- Executive Business Etiquette
- Basic Business Etiquette
- Communication Skills
- Dealing with Difficult People—Communication Skills
- Negotiation Skills
- Business Writing
- Listening Skills
- Communication Skills Training for Technical Professionals
- Communication Skills for Managers and Supervisors
- Workplace Diversity
- Team Building Training Day
- Customer Service
- Telephone Customer Service
- Supervision and Management Skills
- New Supervisor Training
- Coaching for Better Customer Service
- Teambuilding Training Day
- Communication Skills for Managers
- Time Management
- Organizational Skills
- The Polished Administrative Assistant
- Stress Management
- Creativity and Critical Thinking
- Change Management
- Sales Training
- Train the Trainer
- Presentation Skills
- Technical Presentation Skills

Instruments:

- *The Communication Jungle* – A Behavioral Styles Profile

Free Resources at www.businesstrainingworks.com:

- *Creative Icebreakers, Introductions, and Hellos for Teachers, Trainers, and Facilitators*
- *The Benefits of Training*
- *The Trainers' Survival Guide – 25 Proven Exercises to Make Lecture-Based Training Active*

ORDERING INFORMATION:

Business Training Works, Inc.
301-934-3250
www.businesstrainingworks.com

BUSINESS training works | INSPIRE · ENERGIZE · LEARN

NOTES

NOTES

NOTES

NOTES

NOTES

NOTES

NOTES

NOTES

NOTES